FOR THE GOOD

OF ALL, DO

NOT DESTROY

THE BIRDS

For the Good

JENNIFER MOXLEY

# of All, Do

FLOOD EDITIONS

Not Destroy

CHICAGO

the Birds

Published by Flood Editions

www.floodeditions.com

ISBN 978-1-7332734-6-6

Design and composition by Crisis

Printed on acid-free,

recycled paper in Canada

CONTENTS

All the melody that man's ingenuity has ever discovered through the invention of the most exquisite flute can be found in the Nightingale's tiny throat.

—Pliny

Ride it on out like you were a bird

—Marc Bolan

FOR THE GOOD

OF ALL, DO

NOT DESTROY

THE BIRDS

*A*rrested during the implantation of souls at soul number two, the soul of sense, the poet inclines toward the creaturely world. Perhaps it happened thus: the vegetable soul was comfortably placed at the base of the brain and grew up into a tree; the sensual soul flew in secondly and found a perch upon it. Then, for some lost reason, the delicate operation was interrupted. Longing for the third part— the superior and rational soul—the sensual soul started to sing. This beautiful song, "without human meaning / Without human feeling," worked to counter-effect, disorienting the rational soul. It fell into a trance and, much disoriented, began to settle in impossibility. Dreams and desires. Even the language it reputed to order fluttered and flew away.

I have from the first mirrored my "soul of sense" in amphibian skin, feeling always that I was frog-like, and called so by my family, as I was so gay and naïve that facts hit me as disappointments, my half-moon downturned mouth the very pattern of my heart's fret. I could go upon land and water, but I was lighter and happier in the latter. Yet there was something incessantly pecking away inside my mind:

bird information that baffled while portending an entirely other method of sense-knowledge than the one to be gained by sitting in puddles. Restless brooding, you might call it. A plague of wingèd words flying back and forth between the ears.

The periodic escaping of these words in the form of poems muffled the incessant pecking. In the interim I could croak. But a memory still brings a blush: I was far into adulthood when I found myself sitting on the sidelines of a grim little institutional classroom, listening to S. lecture college students on a poem about a bird. I can't remember the poem or the town or the reason for the strange occasion of finding myself among the students with S. as lecturer. But I remember something he said: "When poets speak of birds, they are really talking about themselves." I experienced this seemingly straightforward assertion as I might have the broadcasting of some deeply troubling and intimate secret about myself that I was fearful would be found out.

"We are not chickadees / on a bare limb / with a worm in the mouth," Williams wrote, "The worm is in our brains." It may be, but so is the chickadee that chomps it. The bird in the brain, the song in the throat. Which leads me to wonder if Aristotle oversimplified when laddering up his hierarchy of souls. Are birds considered animals? Are frogs? Shall we decide that the soul who authors the restless brooding known to poets is not just sensual, but singing?

*S*pines are necessary for books and walking. Creeping along. Wings would make things easier. Or would they merely introduce hazards unique to soaring? We all know the mythic warning: Icarus falling into the sea. The spine of my *Complete Poems of Thomas Hardy* is broken in such a way that it falls open to page 150, poem 119: "The Darkling Thrush." Written on 31 December 1900, the very eve of the twentieth century, my century, the one that is fast becoming a shade, this poem is an elegy for the death of the nineteenth. Hardy wrote it when he was sixty. He had twenty-eight years more to live. Years during which, "little cause for carolings" notwithstanding, he would write nearly a thousand poems.

In "The Darkling Thrush" the "fervourless" poet, so spiritually enervated that he cannot support the weight of his bones, looks out upon a devastated winter landscape devoid of music. "[T]angled bine-stems" cut across the sky "Like strings of broken lyres." Gazing at the desolate scene, the poet decides that the "ancient pulse" of a generative life-force has become "shrunken hard and dry." Orpheus has gone underground. What's left behind is post-sexual, emaciated, doddering, Godless, and dead. What could possibly be born of it?

"Full-hearted evensong." The source, an aged thrush: "frail, gaunt, and small, / In blast-beruffled plume" sitting on "bleak twigs." How many missing feathers, broken wings, greasy splattered gray-skinned fragile avian frames can each of us call to mind? Bird carnage abounds in life, yet we rarely encounter it in poems. Hardy's thrush is in tough shape, the bird equivalent of an emaciated Victorian chimney sweep. Those of us born after oil spills became common will doubtless see in him sea birds being soaped down by humans in hazmat suits. But tattered frame and grim surrounds notwithstanding, Hardy's thrush flings forth his soul in a "happy good-night air." The flower will bloom on the bloody battlefield and innocence foment hope in weary experience, but to put such joy in an aged and sickly thing, to deny us all contrast and futures, authors the astonishment of "The Darkling Thrush." Hardy's four stanzas are dreary and sepia from start to finish; no brushstroke of poppy has been painted in to appease the eye, no bluet freaked forth in "dour October."

"Terrestrial things" so described equate to a feeling of soul death. When the thrush's tin-whistle song punctures the haunting dirge of the wind's "death-lament," the poet's bafflement is genuine. He claims to be "unaware" of the font of "blessed Hope" feeding the thrush's song. Yet in "The Darkling Thrush," Hardy—a sixty-year old poet trapped in the desolate landscape of Victorian verse—also flings forth, from the bird soul trapped in his head, a new kind of song: absurd, humorous, ironic, and lost. Existentialist *avant la lettre*. Pure twentieth century.

*I*n Hardy's poem, the landscape qua corpse is male. I imagine his nineteenth century as an English gentleman dressed head to toe in black, magnifying glass turned on the planet, penning shelves of gorgeous prose, stiffly asserting paradigms of "the race," worrying about women and God. I imagine my twentieth century's corpse as American, a "live fast, die young" gender warrior and martyr to fame. Marilyn Monroe or Michael Jackson. The landscape a Crayola flesh-colored late-century development of foreclosed McMansions. Wide streets, big screens, dry lawns. What bird would stop to sing in it? A hermit thrush upon a dumpster in which a homeless person sleeps.

Dumpsters are warm beds to the penniless when desert temperatures fall. I know this because a young poet, for a brief time my student, was crushed to death in a trash truck when the dumpster into which he had crawled to stay warm was emptied into the truck's compacting mechanism. He was heading out west, chasing a bohemian dream. Escaping pain. All who heard the story followed him through the final

Hitchcock's, Baudelaire could gradually zoom into a stuffy overcrowded boudoir to reveal a decapitated woman wearing one pink stocking, her bejeweled head on the night table, and then, just as our minds search with his for what human drama could have possibly resulted in this macabre tableau, introduce a compounding horror: "Did he fulfill his gargantuan desire / on your complaisant inanimate flesh?"

"A Martyr" is an apostrophe to a murder victim, with whom the poet feels sympathy but does not identify. She is somehow, like most of Baudelaire's women, weirdly responsible for having lured from the shadows the Edward Hyde of desire's unconscious. Her sensual body collaborates with its own destruction. But his oeuvre is not lacking in lyric empathy. In "The Albatross" and "The Swan" we are not observers. Humiliated along with these glorious birds, we experience emotions that will never be recollected in or with tranquility. Rather than attempting to match modernity's shocking montage, "The Albatross" and "The Swan" illustrate the way the poem itself can become the therapeutic nightmare. These two grounded birds, wings dragging, feathers in filth, mocked and comical, are pathetic because, although they have been forced out of their natural environment and into our symbolic order, Baudelaire denies them their role as stock figures in the drama of poetic artifice. On their way from mythic symbols to modern metaphors, the birds become trapped in the cruelty of the real. Grounded on the deck of a ship, in the middle of a great city, they are emblems "Of all those who have lost something they may not find / Ever, ever again!"

Baudelaire's birds occasion the realization that Hardy's thrush is perfectly fitted to his circumstances. Matched in his physical dilapidation to his landscape, only his uplifted spirit baffles. How can you, who are so "blast-beruffled," feel joy? Driven by inner stores of song, many are the exiles that have moaned out melodies that assert, time and again, imagination's power to defy the cruelties of fate. Unlike Baudelaire's birds, Hardy's thrush has not been brought down, trapped, or caged. He isn't grounded. Not only his heart but his gaunt, frail body can still fly.

*A*rtifice is the thing most desired by the heart "fastened to a dying animal" in Yeats's "Sailing to Byzantium," its symbol a golden bird. Yet I am surprised to discover that, in a poem I thought I knew well, the word "bird" does not appear in the culminating stanza, where Yeats fantasizes about what his soul might accomplish, "once out of nature." The only time the word appears in "Sailing to Byzantium" is in the opening stanza, pluralized real birds, "in the trees ... at their song." They are irritating the aging poet by recommending the *carpe diem* pleasures of sublunary existence. They are masters in the sensual school of Robert Herrick. "Gather ye rosebuds," these birds seem to sing.

Yeats desires a different education: a metaphysical one. It is an expediency, born out of his realization that "old men" have no role to play in the yearly bacchanal. As a consequence, the aged soul must study not with birds, but with sages who stand in "God's holy fire."

Once the literal birds fly out of the poem, the conundrum of how to sing without them animates the poem's acquisitive quest. A form of singing alights on every stanza. In the second we find the affecting image—imagined by a poet who was robustly handsome in old age—of an aged man as but "A tattered coat upon a stick." Its sonic analog a dull scraping or muted rustle, the static crackle of a radio about to lose its signal. A caesura follows the image and complicates it: "A tattered coat upon a stick, unless . . ."

So much depends upon that "unless"! It is answered by one of my favorite spondee substitutions in English poetry: "unless / Sóul cláp its hands and sing, and louder sing." The singing returns, in vulgar form. The silent soul has become a boisterous fan of "its own magnificence," celebrating "every tatter in its mortal dress."

I find the idea of a soul with "hands" disturbing. A creepy amalgam starts constructing itself out of my David Lynchean image bank. And these immaterial hands make a loud rudimentary music. Something along the lines of the elementary-school stalwart, "If you're happy and you know it clap your hands!" And if you don't know it, must your body go silent? It seems the soul will sing, even in the face of the body's desiccation and death. But Yeats will have none of it. Take me away from all this wretched mortality, he says. I want to be gathered into the "artifice of eternity."

Leaving nature behind, the poet seeks his metaphysical "singing masters" by traveling back in time to "the holy city of Byzantium." The rhetoric of schooling, of divine knowledge as learned, indicates that we are in the presence of mysteries. How does the soul master, not only singing, but aging? Only through artifice. By poem's end the singing is transferred from the natural birds in the trees to the throat of a bird "of hammered gold." This gaudy thing is then "set upon a golden bough to sing / To lords and ladies of Byzantium."

How is this preferable to Hardy's thrush singing to the "the growing gloom"? Does Yeats really wish to be relegated to amusing the aristocracy for all eternity, like some washed-up Las Vegas bard? There is a clue that answers "no." For "such a form as Grecian goldsmith's make" is not set upon a stage, but on a "golden bough," that magic key into Virgil's underworld and metaphor for Orphic knowledge. Yeats has it firmly in his grasp.

He knows the vision in his poem is a fantasy. An arabesque mosaic, intricate, and aesthetically pleasing. A dream solution to an impossible desire, so perfectly expressed elsewhere in his oeuvre: "But O that I were young again / And held her in my arms!" Impossible because, even those in possession of Virgil's key will not unpuzzle death, nor stop the body's decay. Intimations of immortality can only be sent by mortal messengers, such as Hardy's aged frail thrush, who knew as well as Yeats did that to sing for "every tatter in its mortal dress" is the best that any of us dying animals can do.

which grew in memory so dreamlike I half worried I had made it up, that I wrote "Fixed Idea," a poem which would eventually be included in my chapbook *Wrong Life* and my second full-length collection, *The Sense Record*. When "Fixed Idea" came to me I was mildly perturbed to find myself participating in a topos I had mocked: the dead or wounded creature as vehicle through which the poet confronts their own metaphysical questions. It's a move my friends and I had associated with what we dismissively called "mainstream poetry." Richard Eberhart's "The Groundhog" is the most perfect exemplar. In it he loftily travels, mostly in tetrameter, the occasional pentameter reserved for the grander sentiments, from a groundhog "lying dead" "amid the golden fields" to Alexander the Great, Michel de Montaigne, and Saint Teresa "in her wild lament." The journey, which chronicles the decomposition of the groundhog's corpse, takes three years and involves the poet in a series of violent emotions: his senses shake and "waver dim," he feels feverish and trembles, and only his "reverence for knowledge" allows him to "quell the passion of the blood." This reverence, which one might assume a good thing in such a poem, turns American in its anti-intellectualism: it causes him to lose "both love and loathing" for the groundhog's dilemma, earlier expressed in the immortal lines, "Half with loathing, half with a strange love, / I poked him with an angry stick." "Mured up in the wall of wisdom," by the end of the poem he, who had been swept up in the pathos of our "naked frailty" by the "seething cauldron" of the groundhog's being, coldly caps his "withered heart."

Though the groundhog is dead for the entirety of the poem, the cover of my 1951 Chatto & Windus edition of Eberhart's *Selected* is decorated with a line drawing of a startled groundhog, face forward, sitting up on his hind legs, his rabbit-like paws dangling in front of his furry belly. He could scamper right over into a Beatrix Potter book and pass. His dark eyes seem to say: "Can't you save me from Eberhart's poem?"

It has been almost twenty years since I wrote "Fixed Idea," and I needed to reread it to remember how the words unfold. It begins:

> As I move to avoid the bird with his body
> half missing, I gather from his motionless head,
> vibrating eye, he will shelter the truth until the
> final moment . . .

Though in memory I have turned the dreamlike image of the bird at its center into a she-bird, in the poem the bird is gendered male:

> Duty-bound I continue to hock this legitimate
> fallacy until my air socked out turns to sidewalk
> froth, subjective shred, objective truth out cold

there on the phantom wing of the meaning-
lessness that is his struggle, life and very soon now,
death.

The poem says that the bird's death denies my need for "ecstatic release." If this is what I thought the groundhog provided Eberhart, I was wrong. That animal's death only
drove him back into the cold study, to be scrutinized under
Yeats's entombed student lamp. Poetry is the enemy in my
poem, it "pounds in the plank of smug memory," it "funnels
into conformist mallet," but worst of all, it casts "the mythology of personal expression in a seductive / form of
affray." I was working through some things—primarily, my
ambivalence over the political inefficacy of my vocation. I
thought the bird was teaching me that I was under the "obli-
gation of picking one single, totalizing life." But I was
wrong, a single life picks *you*. In grief's wake I felt that
simply living was a form of cruelty. About death neither
demi-bird nor groundhog can help. For that we must turn to
the poem.

*W*hen talk of the nightingale arises, most think of Keats. I think of Creeley. As awkward as an adolescent in a ragged blue sweater, holding a laptop in his extended arms toward the polite faces of my weary students. They lean in to listen. He has downloaded a recording of the nightingale's song from the internet and insists that we hear it. We are Americans and, as everyone knows, the nightingale is not native to the Americas. The technology resists. We watch as this "tattered coat upon a stick"—Creeley is seventy-five at the time—fumbles and frets. Then a faint sound whistles out of the weak speaker on his laptop, tinny and distant. A thinned digital rendition in an institutional setting. This to help us understand the "full-throated ease" of the nightingale's song that inspired Keats to exclaim, "Thou wast not born for death, immortal Bird!"

Though Creeley is an old man, he is hale. His mind sharp, his body nimble. His energy belies the youthful Keats's vision of earthly decrepitude: "Where palsy shakes a few, sad, last gray hairs." Creeley's hair is still full (was it tinted slightly blue?). His salt-and-pepper beard is "soft-coarse," just as I described it in my poem "Little Brick Walk." My cheek tingles from its bristles when he kisses it.

It is 2001 and Ekbert Faas's biography, *Robert Creeley*, has just been published by the University of New England Press. I haven't yet read it, but I know well the controversy. Creeley the wife beater, Creeley the murderously ambitious poet. I am working as an adjunct at the University of Maine. Creeley is a distinguished visiting professor, co-teaching, with S., a course on Black Mountain College in which he spends much of the time reminiscing about old friends and reciting their complex genealogies: Ed Dorn's grandchildren, their spouses, cousins, etc. I'm in that poetic purgatory between one's first book and one's second, made more distressing by the defeat of becoming what I wished to avoid—a teacher. My past threatens to destroy my present in the form of the memoir I've been writing for several years. It bloats more at every sitting, such that I despair of ever finishing. I've published one chapbook, *Wrong Life*. In hopes of understanding my new home state I'm reading Edwin Arlington Robinson.

"Why don't you find a way to talk with Creeley alone?" S. suggests. About poetry. S. knows I'm struggling. Though I feel close to the work and comfortable with the man, I'm terrified of being alone with him. Of his awkwardness, and of my own. We plan the coffee date, though it's clear we both dread it.

There's a dampness that fogs up the large windows of the library café. The university's collection of beer steins, honoring alum Rudy Vallée's rendition of Maine's "Stein Song," stares gaudily out of its glass case. Creeley and I settle into a small round table next to a wall. Did I make some falsely naïve query, such as, "How does one go on being a poet?" When Creeley had first arrived on campus he had pointedly said to me, "It would be nice if you could *survive.*" I took him to mean my work: it would be nice if your work could survive. Advice may have been solicited in that stuffy, humid, room, but what came back was pure confession. Creeley settled into an agonized ramble, an *apologia* for his behavior toward women. "I never hit anyone," he said. His eye linoleum aimed. My fingers nervously folded the lip of my paper cup.

"What / was that great poem about *the man against // the sky*"? asked the poet in "Old Poems," from *Life and Death.* The copy S. and I have on our shelf is signed: "¡Wow! With pleasure, indeed— Paris 1998." The answer is, of course, the title poem of E. A. Robinson's 1916 volume *The Man against the Sky,* a poem I had just been reading a few weeks before Creeley hoped to impress upon my students the import of the nightingale's song.

Robinson's is a poem of pained existential questioning,

which ends upon "the cold eternal shores / That look sheer down / To the dark tideless floods of Nothingness / Where all who know may drown." Questioning whether we should fear "the soul's dead end in death," Robinson joins poetic understanding to the knowledge of the "terrors that began / When Death let fall a feather from his wings / And humbled the first man." Death as a bird, though hardly "easeful."

The central image in Robinson's poem is the silhouette of a man on the top of a hill with the sun blazing behind him. He could be a Zarathustra, a giant, or a lost soul. The ambiance shades toward *Götterdämmerung*. As I sat with Creeley —one of my poet gods—and heard his confession, an envy grew in me. In "Little Brick Walk" I wrote it thus:

> How I envied him.
> Freed from impatience
> by ample time, no longer admonished by
> desire. But most of all
> I envied him
> those many husbanded years,
> perplexed to rhyme
> by her alien life . . .

(I think now that I must have lifted that usage of "alien" from Keats's unforgettable image of the Biblical Ruth listening to the nightingale's melodious strains "amid the alien corn.") I envied that Creeley—unlike Keats, whose youth grew "spectre-thin" and died—had lived long enough to have the question of whether or not his poems would survive answered. But most of all I envied him the care of his wives. While rarely uncoupled, overlapping as he did from one wife to the next, there was something lonely about him. Like Robinson's man against the sky, Creeley often seemed to me, for all his talk of company, "alone up there . . . as if he were the last god going home / Unto his last desire."

I see S.'s dissertation advisor, Marxist scholar Neil Lazarus, leaning back in his chair, putting his hand to his freckled forehead and proclaiming, with South African cadence, "A drowsy numbness pains my sense, as though of hemlock I had drunk!" Had he drunk one too many Labatt "Blues," the cheap Canadian lager we had on offer during our weekly poker games? Whatever prompted this performance, Neil's dramatic recitation was a testimonial to the Nightingale ode's reputation as catalog of High Romantic moves. And indeed, I can't but marvel at how Keats's "viewless wings of Poesy" remain in flight despite numerous balance checks through the turbid winds of bathos. How did he manage to include "pards," "fays," "magic casements," and "faery lands," and still make us think about nothing but death? Perhaps the music of the poem, like that of the bird, drugs the reader?

The fame of Keats's ode obscures all other nightingale poems. It is the one. So much so that I've never accepted that scene near the end of John Huston's version of *The Dead* (not in Joyce's story) when Miss O'Callaghan asks tenor Bartell

D'Arcy if the nightingale's song is "like in the ode of Mr. Keats" and he says, with a seducer's motivated twinkle in his eye, "Not at all." What does he mean "not at all"? How can that be? Does the hallucinatory artifice of the poem's nightingale put static in the channel of both the poet's senses and the real bird's song? Keats attempts no homonymic representation of his auditory experience, as did medieval poets who heard in the nightingale's music a springtime call to battle: *oci! oci!* (kill! kill!). Concerned more with its effects, Keats tells us only that the bird's song is about "summer," and sung "full-throated" in "ecstasy." It is both "high requiem" and "plaintive anthem." With the possible exception of the first two descriptors, we're soundly in the realm of pathetic fallacy.

A contradiction arises in the poem when Keats proclaims, "Now more than ever seems it rich to die, / To cease upon the midnight with no pain," but then he quickly realizes that, were that richness to overtake him, the music would end: "Still wouldst thou sing, and I have ears in vain— / To thy high requiem become a sod." In his sonnet "Bright Star" Keats articulates the inverse, the desire to *live* forever in a moment of ecstasy: "to feel for ever" his "fair love's ripening breast." Scholar Michael Clune sees in this Keats's desire "for the complete arrest of neurobiological time." The romantic scene Keats wants never to end in "Bright Star" is tranquil, G-rated. He is "Pillow'd upon" his "fair love's ripening breast." Quite the sleepy lover's idle when placed beside the well-nigh pornographic frenzy he's aroused to in the Nightingale ode. The bird's song drives him to a macabre, almost Baudelairean desire to coo sweet nothings into death's ear, asking him "To take into the air my quiet breath." The perversity of this climax hedged (haven't we all played this game?) by the disclaimer at the poem's end: "Was it a vision, or a waking dream? / Fled is that music: —Do I wake or sleep?"

Another contradiction at the heart of Keats's ode is that the nightingale, while having provided a bittersweet accompaniment to human trials, woes, and passions since "ancient days," yet remains ignorant of them. This "light-winged Dryad of the trees" "hast never known / The weariness, the fever, and the fret" of human existence, "Where but to think is to be full of sorrow." Despite the ode's glut of classical and medieval mythic allusions, the bird at its center remains just a bird, far from the *Philomela querens* (nightingale lamenting) motif that emerged from one of Ovid's most heartbreaking metamorphosis stories to flutter its way through Western literature for the next two thousand years. Removing the bird from its darker mythic associations with rape, mutilation, and infanticide, Keats's ode lent itself nicely to Neil Lazarus's melodramatic quotations of emotional extremes, which no self-respecting postmodernist would actually admit to feeling.

The nightingale is lamenting, but for what or whom? For the loss of her virginity, her voice, her homeland, her children, her lover. Though in nature it is the male bird who sings through twilight and into the darkness, in poetry the bird is almost always female. The story of Tereus, Procne, and Philomela as told by Ovid in Book VI of his *Metamorphoses* is the common seed. Tereus, a Thracian king, rapes Philomela, the sister of his Athenian wife Procne, then cuts out her tongue to hide the crime. Ovid provides a racial explanation for Tereus's actions, telling us that he is spurred on by "an inborn tribal urge." The violated sister weaves her story into a tapestry. The sisters collude against the Thracian. They murder Procne's son Itys, then roast and feed him to his father. Enraged to have been made "the miserable tomb of his own son," Tereus unsheathes his sword and lunges toward the Athenian women. It is at this moment that all three players in the brutal drama grow feathers. The war-thirsty Tereus becomes a hoopoe bird, with a helmet-like crest. All Ovid tells us about Philomela's and Procne's bird selves is that one "wings her way into the dark woods," while

25

the other "rises to the roof." The myth was Greek, dating back at least five hundred years, and his audience didn't need to be told that Procne became a nightingale and Philomela a swallow. They knew. As my tattered edition of Edith Hamilton has it, "Procne into a nightingale . . . [because of] all the birds her song is sweetest because it is saddest. She never forgets the son she killed," and "Philomela into a swallow which, because her tongue was cut out, only twitters and can never sing."

Quantifying sadnesses between these particular sisters seems to fall rather short of fair, and indeed, most poets in the English tradition switch the metamorphoses and give the name Philomela to the nightingale. Hamilton blames the Roman poets for this confusion. After calling Ovid "inconceivably bad" for having "described in fifteen long lines how Philomela's tongue was cut out and what it looked like as it lay 'palpitating' on the earth," she adds that these idiot Romans "got the sisters confused and said that the tongueless Philomela was the nightingale, which was obviously absurd." That a tongueless woman could grow feathers and shrink to the size of a tiny-boned bird, on the other hand, is perfectly credible.

Though Hamilton objects to Ovid's lingering over the brutality of Philomela's mutilation on aesthetic grounds, I suspect she was of the Victorian school of propriety that preferred silence when it came to "unpleasantness." Silence or substitution. Some might call it collusion. In Ovid, bird similes permeate the description of the rape scene. Tereus is described as an eagle with "eyes . . . fixed on his helpless prize," Philomela as a "a shuddering dove whose feathers are now drenched in its own blood." The brutality detailed by Ovid becomes in Hamilton an exchange of false words: "Tereus told Philomela that he had received news of Procne's death and he forced her into a pretended marriage." The bit about Procne's death is pure fabrication on Hamilton's part, added to explain Philomela's "surrender" to Tereus. The deceived maiden is then chided for being "ill-advised enough to threaten" Tereus, which leads him to cut out her tongue, after which (though Hamilton leaves this out) he "again, again, gave free rein to his lust / upon that mangled body."

Hamilton blames the Romans for the misattribution of the birds, but perhaps medieval poets were also motivated by the beauty of the word "Philomela." Though etymologically more likely to have derived from "lover of apples" (philos + mêlon), who would be blamed for assuming it to mean "lover of song" (philos + mélo)? And so it has been "folk-etymologized," according to the Latin Wiktionary, at least since the *Metamorphoses*. I find a kind of bittersweetness in the thought that the gods would have given a woman robbed of speech the power of a song so moving that it could

*U*nlike Philomela and Procne, Orpheus's betrothed, the dryad Eurydice, is fated to remain a "still unravish'd bride." Mere hours after her wedding ceremony she is whisked into the underworld, the victim of a snakebite. The story is well known. Her untimely death becomes a pretext for the poet to challenge divine orders. Overwhelmed by grief, the newlywed grabs his lyre and heads into the realm of the dead on a mission to retrieve his bride. He plays sweetly and seduces the shades with his song. Persephone convinces Hades to let Orpheus take Eurydice back into the upper world. But there is a condition. On their journey out of darkness, Orpheus must not look at Eurydice. One glance, and the deal is off. When he violates this taboo, he consigns his bride to die yet again.

In Ovid's version, Eurydice responds to the poet's failure with "one final, faint 'Farewell'— / so weak it scarcely reached [Orpheus's] ears." In Virgil's fourth *Georgic* she's given more eloquence: "Orpheus," she begins, "we are ruined, you and I! / What utter madness is this?" She explains what is happening to her disbelieving spouse:

> See, once again
> The cruel Fates are calling me back and darkness
> Falls on my swimming eyes. Goodbye for ever.
> I am borne away wrapped in an endless night,
> Stretching to you, no longer yours, these hands,
> These helpless hands.

As she thins into a shade, the poet is left grasping at shadows, sentenced to remain a mortal shattered by his "shock experience."

The loss is so devastating it sunders Orpheus from society. For seven months, Virgil tells us, Orpheus wept, "alone in the wild," wandering "over icy steppes / Of the farthest north." During these months he becomes a true poet. Having been lessoned out of the hubristic contention that his music might overturn divine law, he becomes one with the "lower animal," which Aristotle placed outside of politics and the realm of the rational soul. Orpheus's sensual soul sings his tale of woe, entrancing tigers and moving oak trees.

If we could hear such music, what would it sound like? According to Virgil, like a "nightingale / Mourning beneath the shade of a poplar-tree," lamenting "lost young ones whom a heartless ploughman / Has spied unfledged in the nest and plundered." The male poet whose overconfidence made a promise of false hope to the woman he loved becomes, through metaphor, a she-bird mourning her lost chicks. Both human and bird story unfold as a result of male violence. In Ovid, Eurydice dies from a snakebite, a blameless accident. In Virgil we learn that the "poor doomed girl" was bitten by a snake in a state of panic when fleeing the would-be rapist Aristaeus. The "heartless ploughman" and Aristaeus are one and the same, men who do damage to satisfy hungers. Just like Tereus.

For all the beauty of his music, when Orpheus was in the underworld he was no better than the nightingale in the hawk's talons as described by Hesiod: "though you are a great chanteuse," says the hawk, "I can have you for dinner, or let you go, if I wish, for only fools oppose their betters in strength." Fool that Orpheus was to think he could undo death, his violation of the taboo placed upon him was fated. For even the poet who can keep a "drowsy Emperor awake" or charm the King of the Dead is still but a nightingale in the grip of a hawk. However beautiful the poet's song, should it displease, it will be squelched as surely as Philomela's tongue was cut from her mouth. "[I]f I'm shut up in these woods," she threatens Tereus, "I'll shout / unto the trees; I'll move the rocks to pity!" She has undergone an experience so heinous as to have acquired an Orphic inheritance. Her story will stir even the dumb, sensual world. Tereus meets her boast not with freedom, or the death she longs for, but with censorship, a bloody precursor to the "non-disclosure agreement." Her tongue, once cut from her body, murmurs as faintly as Ovid's Eurydice, already having joined the realm of the dead. Yet truth will out—at least in myth. Philomela, denied the power of speech, becomes an artist of the loom and names her abuser in cloth.

Orpheus, too, will be mutilated by Thracian anger—women, in this case (were they also spurred, as Ovid said of Tereus, by an "inborn tribal urge"?). His body is torn apart and his head severed. Yet unlike Philomela's poor voiceless tongue, the male poet's head maintains its song even after decapitation. On its journey down the Hebrus river, it moans in haunting syllables the name "Eurydice!" It is a lament that, like the nightingale's song, will be heard "far and wide" and fill "all the air with grief."

$\mathcal{M}$ust a woman be sentenced to endless night for a poet to be born? A woman or a she-bird. "*For I am almost sure I see her dimly whichever way I look*," sings the grieving he-bird in Whitman's bildungsroman "Out of the Cradle Endlessly Rocking." The bird is cast in the role of Orpheus, a grieving lover and poet mourning the loss of his Eurydice. The boy protagonist of Whitman's poem has no Eurydice but his innocence, which is lost to him through the snakebite of death: the death of a female bird. The "curious boy" had been spying upon a sweet domestic scene: two birds and their nest, filled with "four light-green eggs spotted with brown." Then "one forenoon" he notices that the she-bird is gone. "Nor return'd that afternoon, nor the next, / Nor ever appear'd again." In the wake of the she-bird's presumed death, the boy as witness translates the "reckless despairing carols" of the he-bird, whose eye, in the disbelief born of the shock of grief, becomes a lens of pure longing, projecting his mate against the dramatic backdrop of the umbrageous landscape. He sees her as that "*little black thing*" "*fluttering out among*" the white of the breaking waves, as that "*dusky spot*" upon the brown yellow of the "*Low-hanging moon.*" The magical incantation of the avian Orpheus's lament throws the boy translator into an ecstatic animism: against the light of an enlarged yellow half-moon dipping down into the moaning ocean he finds himself barefoot in the waves. The atmosphere "dall[ies]" with his hair and his heart bursts forth with a love "long pent." "[S]trange tears" course down his cheeks. His innocence dies and his bird soul awakens and begins to sing:

> Demon or bird! (said the boy's soul,)
> Is it indeed toward your mate you sing? Or is it really
>   to me?
> For I, that was a child, my tongue's use sleeping, now I
>   have heard you,
> Now in a moment I know what I am for, I awake,
> And already a thousand singers, a thousand songs, clearer,
>   louder and more sorrowful than yours,
> A thousand warbling echoes have started to life within
>   me . . .

Whitman describes his newly born bird soul as a "sweet hell within." In it he must forevermore reside, never to return to his previous innocence. No more could Orpheus bring Eurydice back than Whitman's once "peaceful child" state return once he has been called to his vocation. The Thracian

34

singer's hubristic mission only serves to revivify Eurydice's hopes to live, not her actual life, just as Whitman's boast of being a "chanter of pains and joys" and "uniter of here and hereafter" only allows him to revivify the *loss* of his innocence, not the untrammeled state itself. That can never be brought back, except symbolically through the lyric poem, which uses "powerful feelings recollected in tranquility" to conjure the original emotion: "A man, yet by these tears a little boy again." Through the lyric poem the ritual of loss and rebirth—"like some old crone rocking the cradle"—may begin again.

"Out of the Cradle" is a backward glance. A second death of innocence. The mature poet is a lover and psychopomp and the author of all of our songs. And yet his powers cannot protect him from being shredded and reformed again by a mere word. The "clew" he is given by the sea, a "savage old mother"—the key, the knowledge, which even Orpheus could not vanquish—is, of course, death. "Low and delicious," Whitman calls it, before the final five-beat incantation: "Death, death, death, death, death."

Which returns me to my opening question. Must a female, whether woman or bird, die for a poet to be born? Must Eurydice and the she-bird die that "never more the cries of unsatisfied love be absent" from the lyric poet? Orpheus's song was changed by death. It became so powerful it aroused the murderous anger of the Thracian women who, as Virgil put it, "Tore him apart . . . and strewed his limbs / Over the countryside." Eurydice's death looks quick and gentle by comparison. And from the shredding of Orpheus . . . Sappho, and the whole of the lyric tradition.

No longer needful of the mythic parable to explain the inexplicable, in *Song of Myself* Whitman writes as if directly to Orpheus:

> Were mankind murderous or jealous upon you, my
> brother, my sister?
> I am sorry for you, they are not murderous or jealous
> upon me,
> All has been gentle with me, I keep no account with
> lamentation,
> (What have I to do with lamentation?)

Whitman's rejection of lamentation seems slightly disingenuous, even given his attempts to refigure the lyric tradition's origin in death as "eternal life" and "happiness." As his oeuvre reasserts repeatedly, "I do not ask the wounded person how he feels, I myself become the wounded person." But there is no need of angry Bacchantes to bequeath Whitman's song to the next poet. Though self-fashioned as an original, he was born into his ancient inheritance. It allows him to will his own *sparagmos*, a transcendental metamorphosis through death's embrace to the whole: "I bequeath myself to the dirt to grow from the grass I love." Whitman strews himself over the countryside, that we may find him, as he assures us, under our boot-soles.

Edwin Fussell, the eccentric Catholic dandy who, through the vehicle of "General Literature 6B: Understanding Poetry," introduced me to "Out of the Cradle Endlessly Rocking," did so by stressing the poem's structural indebtedness to Italian opera. Though I had but a passing knowledge of opera, I was pleased to learn of this key into the poem because, scant concert-going experience aside, "opera lover" was a descriptor well matched to the slightly outdated pretense and old-world formality I cultivated as a youth. Like an opera, the poem has an overture introducing the poem's motifs—the twenty-line hyperbaton that opens the poem, ending with: "A reminiscence sing." The overture is followed by a sequence of "arias" sung by the he-bird and indicated by italics which alternate with the boy's recitative. This makes so much sense to me now, given that the first three Renaissance musical works we have come to call "operas" all took the myth of Orpheus and Eurydice as their subject matter. Opera is, after all, a musical form that creates a theatrical mirror-world in which humans communicate, court, and grieve in song. Just like the birds.

*A*lmost as if countering Whitman's five "deaths," Denise Levertov ends her poem "Claritas" with five instances
of the word "light":

> Sun
> light.
>> Light
> light light light.

Staring at this cluster of "lights" I see the strangeness of the
residual "gh." I feel I can hear that Middle English "g" assert
itself anew. The repetition also erodes the word's meaning,
allowing its sound to transform into something more like
music or birdsong. And indeed, "Claritas" is a poem about a
bird, a "whitethroated sparrow," the imagination of whose
song Levertov uses to define her own creative process; he is
"the artist," as is she. She refers to the sparrow as the "All-
Day Bird," a pointed counter to the poetically celebrated
nightingale, who is also her fellow Briton. Yet, while the
nightingale has not migrated to the New World, Levertov

has. She is in America now, and her poems, as well as the birdsong she hears, are shaped by a new-world cadence.

Levertov's "All-Day Bird" works on his song like an earnest Puritan looking for signs of predestination, "striving" by the bright light of "Claritas"—Latin for clarity and brightness—"in hope" and "good faith." Her description of the sparrow's process qualifies him for co-author credit of her 1965 essay, "Some Notes on Organic Form." The bird wants to make his song "ever more precise, closer / to what he knows." "There is the proposition / and the develop-ment," the poem goes on, "The way / one grows from the other"—

> May the first note
> be round enough
> and those that follow
> fine, fine as
> sweetgrass,
> 　　prays
> the All-Day Bird.

Levertov's choice of the word "prays" sustains the theological reading. Yes, the bird is an artist, but to follow her essay's claim that the poet should "discover and reveal" the "form in all things" requires a bit of grace. Or, as Levertov's emendation to Creeley's dictum would have it: "Form is never more than a *revelation* of content." The substitution of "revelation" for "extension" assures a god's involvement. The "beginning of the fulfillment" of the *demand* of the poem, "Some Notes" asserts, "is to contemplate," which comes from *templum,* meaning temple, and thus "means, not simply to observe, to regard, but to do these things in the presence of a god."

Once the All-Day Bird makes his prayer, the poem returns to the mundane. A sequence of images from the natural world are followed by microscopic measures of ideational intervals. Both bird and poet want their songs to be as fine as a lizard's tail, a chive leaf, the *"shadow of a difference"* or *"hair's breadth"* between note and note. The penultimate stanza is descriptive:

> The dew is on the vineleaves.
> My tree
> is lit with the
> break of day.

It is not clear who is speaking here, bird or poet. "My tree": I suppose a bird on a branch could think of that residence, however temporary, as a kind of possession. Or could this tree, all aglow with the dawn, be the poplar from Levertov's short prose piece, "Say the Word"—which appears five pages after "Claritas" in her 1964 book *O Taste and See*? That poplar—her tree—ostentatiously grows on the northeast horizon of the property of her new home in Temple, Maine. A tree "tall enough to block off almost all of that swooping valley among the nearer hills beyond which lay the far-away mountains she longed to see."

One night, after supper with her husband and son, she suggests they might cut down this poplar to satisfy her desire for a view. Despite the twilight hour, her husband immediately takes up the charge with the gusto of a man vitalized by an opportunity to do his wife's bidding. As man and boy head off to the edge of the property to confront the obstructive poplar, the woman, remaining by the house, stands "looking at the tree." "The sun was just gone down, in back of her, but the eastern sky, which had clouded over while they were indoors, was not yet dark ... As she looked, a rift in the clouds gave to the poplar's topmost branches a last gleam of sunlight ..." The wind ripples through the poplar's leaves, which "even in the dulled light flickered like sequins."

As she contemplates the tree's silhouette her commitment to its destruction begins to waver. "She had spoken so quickly," the woman thinks, "and at once these actions began." She had spoken, but now she finds herself unable to speak. Though she desires the stay, thoughts of her husband prevent her from issuing it: "Could she—with her persistent sense of the precariousness of happiness, the knife-edge balance of his confidence, of all sureness—could she run to him now with a plea to stop what she had begun? To stop, when it was as much out of concern for her needs as for any need of his own to see those particular mountains, that he was felling this tree?" She stands mute, listening to the "thwocks" of the axe that broadcast through the twilight the tree's destruction. Only when her son cries out "Now!" as the tree finally falls is the spell broken. She begins to run toward the doomed poplar but catches her foot and stumbles. She stops, dumbfounded, "a feeling of loneliness and confusion overwhelming her."

The allusion to Gerard Manley Hopkins's "Binsey Poplars" is palpable:

> Ten or twelve, only ten or twelve
> Strokes of havoc unselve
> The sweet especial scene

She was thinking of Hopkins when she wrote "Say the Word," and she was thinking of Hopkins when she wrote "Some Notes on Organic Form." She invokes his conception of "inscape" as an example of the intrinsic form she feels the poet must work carefully—through contemplation and meditation—to reveal. There is a passivity in this poetic, a *tracing* or *following*: "from that moment of being let in to the possibility of the poem" the poet must let the "experience lead him through the world of the poem, its unique inscape revealing itself as he goes." Just as the All-Day Bird allows the development of his song to grow from its proposition.

Against this passivity, how then to read the final stanza of "Claritas"?

> Sun
> light.
> Light
> light light light.

We can move between noun and verb, turning the light into a bird "lighting" upon a branch, or see Levertov *verbing* the noun as Hopkins does in his poem "Peace": "When, when, Peace, will you, Peace?" Either way the imperative mood, the very opposite of *tracing* or *following,* sets the tone. Perhaps the medieval Christian use of *claritas* as *claritas Dei*, the light of God—so different from Whitman's dark Orphic knowledge—gives a clue. The power of the word. *Fiat lux.* Let there be light. Let "Sun / light. / Light / light light light."

*P*rose is the fool's gold that fails to cage the poet, or so asserts Emily Dickinson in poem 445: "They shut me up in Prose –." To shut something up: "To place or store away in a closed box; to keep from view or use; to confine within bounds," but also, by the nineteenth century, "To cause to stop talking, to reduce to silence" (OED). The poem goes on to compare the futility of shutting the poet up to lodging a bird in a pound, *for treason*. Absurd. Likewise, civic betrayals have no meaning for the avian logics by which a bird soul abides. The poet's prose-break is fated by the jailor's ignorance of her nature. Girl nature, bird soul. Despite the impossibility of doing so, both will be cuffed repeatedly. Shut up. The body confined in a failed attempt to control the mind.

Who would do such a heartless thing? The socially sanctified faceless "they." The unbroken policing authority that runs from parent to teacher to publisher to state. All who would redraw the lyrical circle into a narrative box:

> They shut me up in Prose –
> As when a little Girl
> They put me in the Closet –
> Because they liked me "still" –

Following this evocation of shutting the girl poet into a closet to quiet her—a sort of grim Victorian-era "time out" —Dickinson creates an ambiguous adjective to adverb hinge with the word "still":

> Still! Could themself have peeped –
> And seen my Brain – go round –
> They might as wise have lodged a Bird
> For Treason – in the Pound –

This is Dickinson's analogical point: the poet, like the bird, is not subject to your laws, impossible to jail. And the failing of the "they" is manifestly about a limit of insight and curiosity, but latently linguistic. If "they" could *peep*, like a bird or poet, they wouldn't be so foolish as to lock girls in closets, birds in prisons, or poets in prose.

You can shut me up, but "Die Gedanken sind frei" (*thoughts are free*). Or so goes the old German protest song. But it is not so simple. Dickinson's final stanza creates a puzzle. The bird lodged in the pound, "Himself":

> . . . has but to will
> And easy as a Star
> Look down opon Captivity –
> And laugh – No more have I –

All it takes to soar above and laugh at one's captivity is *will*. But what does it mean to be "easy as a Star"? Is she merely saying that the heights of the bird soul are such that it effortlessly condescends to human restraints? Or is Dickinson saying that what the "they" can't understand is that both bird and poet are *with* the stars—from the Latin *con* (with) + *sidera* (stars). They are *considerers,* subject to none but stellar logics.

*T*he night before Valentine's Day, I awoke into what had become a rather typical nocturnal state of bodily boil over and knew myself to be a bird. A human-sized white dove. I could feel my wings wrapped over and around my strong white egg-of-a-chest. My feet were scaly and taloned and when I stretched them, they felt good. The sounds: my feathers, my quiet soft chest, the rustling mechanism of my wings, were especially present to me. I could imagine, with very little effort, what it would feel like to raise my wings up over my back and press them down through the resistance of the air in an effort to fly. A few times, they pulled me up from the bed with almost frightening force. Still a novice, I lurched with little control. Yet I managed to be airborne at least once—blue skies, roof tops. Soon I grew frightened by the height. Everything funneled back into my body in the sheets. On my back, wings wrapped around me, my eyes black beads, my quick and nervous head quite still. The metamorphosis was so palpable my fear arose in the form of a cage. How unbearable it would be. Those awful confines.

The best part of this avian metamorphosis was the comfort. I felt so calm and peaceful, so safe. My wings were cool and fragile yet felt sturdy and powerful. They could hold me close and they could take me away, up into the ether. I was all bird. Dove self.

I had never lived alone before. At least not for long. There had been an aborted attempt when I first tried to go away to college, best forgotten. My mother's nostalgia for those few years in her twenties when she lived in San Francisco and worked as a secretary for McGraw Hill had nevertheless imbued the idea of "a single working girl in a flat" with edgy aplomb. But she hadn't lived alone. Not if you count Dirty Eddie. And how could you not? Dirty Eddie (never spoken of without his epithet) was legendary. A budgerigar with a filthy vocabulary and a penchant for highballs, Dirty Eddie was my mother's cherished companion in her little studio apartment. The few photographs I have from that brief window between my mother's flight from El Paso and her wedlock to my father are weirdly miniature, as if she could only afford small prints. The people in them are thin and overdressed, usually with a drink in hand. The women's hairdos curl away from their faces, the men's glasses reflect the light. Who are these people? In one snapshot, my mother sits on the edge of a bed and looks down at a box in her lap wrapped with a bow. She has a flower in her hair, and her elegant, long legs are crossed beneath her skirt. She wears dark, thick, high-heeled shoes, like those worn by pinups on the fuselage of fighter planes. There is only one photo featuring Dirty Eddie. He is perched on the edge of a glass, unaware of the camera. The picture is a little square, maybe two and a half by two and a half, and with a wide white border. In that silent monochrome image, Eddie looks like a normal, unremarkable bird.

For some reason I always imagined him as blue. Blue seemed like the color of a bird called Dirty Eddie. This is why, not long after I moved into my first real single girl's flat on Eighth Street, right in the heart of San Diego's Hillcrest neighborhood, I bought a blue budgie. Under the sway of Jean-Jacques Rousseau's romantic thought, I named him "Emile." It was appropriate insofar as he managed to remain a "natural bird" in the "cage" of human society. When I told my mother I thought of Emile as "my Dirty Eddie," she smiled. "But Dirty Eddie was green," she said, disrupting my long-held image.

At first my apartment was stark and, but for the full-length mirror left behind by Amy, my former boss and some-time lover, bare. Onto that gold-framed mirror Amy had affixed a very small sticker of Burt, from Sesame Street's "Burt and Ernie," wearing a dress and a blond wig. "See, it's

Burt in drag," she said, the entirety of her adorable waxen face seeming to wink as if to say, "get it?"

Emile also had a mirror. His mirror was a little purse mirror, which I had attached to the golden cage bars at one end of his high, blond-wood perch with an old rubber band. He spent most of his time in front of it, very earnestly and excitedly chatting, wooing, and sometimes fighting with his own reflection. I too spent many hours in front of my mirror. I preened and judged and adjusted. And though I did not take my reflection for another being entirely, there were times when the gaze she returned was so alien that I suspected Amy's gift a portal to the unconscious, periodically sending back an evanescent portrait showing just how fearful and sad I really was.

My mother was dying. I knew that this was "true" in the way that a child knows that she shouldn't do something because it is dangerous without any real understanding of *what* the danger really consists of. Life in the wake of the transgression is unthinkable, and therefore, is not thought.

In the months I lived on my own with Emile, I came to appreciate what a comfort Dirty Eddie must have been to my mother. Parakeets greet you when you come home. They bob and chirp and run from one end of the perch to the other with excitement. As soon as I returned from work I would open up Emile's cage and he, as I had trained him to do, would jump onto my finger and stretch his black-and-white "newspaper head" out for a beak-to-lip peck. If I ate Jack in the Box at my little kitchen table, he would make a skid landing on the Formica in hopes of tugging a piece of wilted lettuce off my bacon cheeseburger. He joined my Smith Corona electric typewriter in symphonic bombast as I typed up my stream-of-conscious responses to Jean-Jacques Rousseau's *Du contrat social* or tried my hand at dramatic monologue.

I had read that birds see the human trunk as a tree, with arms for branches and the head as a bird sitting at its apex. I thought of this each time Emile flew to my shoulder, pulled at my earring, or nestled into a tangle of unkempt hair. During such intimacies I stilled the urge to heed the call of Orpheus and walk my roots about the room, though not on Emile's account. If he indeed thought me to be a tree, he had no issue with my mobility.

So much more satisfying than the company of radio or TV, Emile responded and had clearly expressed views. He preferred Baroque music over 80s pop, millet between meals, and visited his unselfconscious lust—in a vulgar habit which I imagined Dirty Eddie also indulged—upon all gold and shiny things. He was a truly joyful companion.

In those early days I did not suspect that Emile, like poor drunk Elpenor, would not make it past Circe's ingle. His robust *joie de vivre* belied his fragility. When we packed up our little *ménage à deux* and moved in with S., Emile adapted well to the new arrangement, considering. "He thinks you're his mate," S. would say. Though I didn't argue with this notion, the use of the word "mate" discomfited me. I preferred to think of our bond in another way. If I was his arboreal proxy, he was the imp of my autonomy.

Just as Dirty Eddie had been for my mother. How, I wonder, did she transport her soused companion to Mexico when she moved there to live with my father once they had, against her own mother's wishes, married in a civil (not Catholic) ceremony? I never asked myself this question, not even when S. and I transported Emile from California to Rhode Island in a tinny ten-foot U-Haul. By this point we had adopted a sleek black kitten, who suffered the journey in a carrier at my feet. Emile, cage accustomed, had a better time of it, placed high up next to my head and chirping the length of the continent.

Did Dirty Eddie take a Pan Am flight, or was he stuffed into the back of a station wagon? Whatever his mode of international travel, I imagine he welcomed the trade of a single girl's small flat in silver gray San Francisco for a balmy sunlit mid-century abode in azure Mazatlán. But Dirty Eddie's stint in paradise would not last long. One of the several "girls" my parents had in to cook and wash and clean had left something open: a window, a door, some way into the wider world which, either from fear or the desire for freedom, Dirty Eddie took, flying out of my mother's life for good.

Over this loss she never calmed. The probably well-meaning "girl" was stupid, neglectful, even malicious, my father unsympathetic. When, after fourteen years of marriage, my father declared "I haven't loved you for seven," the loss of Dirty Eddie was recast as an early warning sign that my mother's sacrifice of autonomy to matrimony had been mistaken from the first. The strange foreign people who surrounded the young wife were careless of the things she cared for.

"These little creatures mean so much to us," she wrote to me when Emile died. My body shook. My tears fell on the card, a beautiful Japanese print. A tree, stilled. It was winter in Rhode Island, cold and gray. The previous week Emile had been out of his cage, doing laps around the bedroom when our sleek black kitten, now a svelte and gorgeous cat, leapt some four feet off the bed and sliced open his abdomen. We had grown lax. Circe and Emile had lived together for over a year without incident. Had she had been lying in wait all along? Graveled by this unnatural "great chain of being" household?

The wound did not kill the bird. He was breathing. I was desperate. S. called around and found an avian vet. But his office was far away and our car had no heat. New in town and with few friends, we called our landlord for help. I can't imagine what Oldatino—a handsome, Portuguese man with a beautiful wife and several adorable children—thought when we asked if we could borrow his car to take our bird to the emergency room. But he agreed.

Our efforts failed. After an operation on his intestine, Emile stayed overnight at the vet. Unable to screw up the courage to ask our landlord for a car loan again, when we went to pick up Emile, we fitted his travel cage with a hot water bottle and wrapped it with a flannel blanket. He made it all the way back home, but he died a few hours later.

After his death our shabby apartment with its worn rugs and cheap bookshelves seemed to center around the empty cage. I could no longer pretend that I did not know what the danger really consisted of. Emile was gone and I would have to live without him. Just as I would have to live without my mother, very soon indeed and for the rest of my life.

*F*or the first twelve years of my life I shared a room. Except for the jeopardy of constant surveillance this arrangement was not onerous, yet it was enough to make me romanticize solitude. I thought, if alone, really and truly, I might detect something concerning my essential being that I couldn't hear through the perfectly curated teasing and boisterous din of my brothers. But I was ill-suited to solitude. This is why it took me so very long to settle into my vocation. Reading and writing seemed, on the surface, to require such quiet. Now in midlife I've come to delight in solitude, but only in small doses and when safely cushioned. I have discovered what male writers have known for centuries: the pleasure of a study's closed door through which you can still hear the hum of your household. Not Rilke's "two solitudes" that "protect and border and greet each other," but the cover of real companionship to keep me from falling irretrievably into a well of words. Though I am still imaginatively drawn to the idea of the devotional soul that retreats or, like an anchorite, seals herself away from the world in service to the page, in practice such isolation is injurious to my happiness.

Solitude in service to the page made Flaubert miserable too. "He had spent the greater part of his adult life in ... solitude ... largely because he preferred to devote his energies almost exclusively to literature," writes Robert Baldick, translator of Flaubert's last completed work, *Three Tales*. "Yet his books brought him little satisfaction." Flaubert's devotion to his art was a sort of mania that turned his vocation into a willed thing, a skill one could apprentice to and labor at, seeking the perfection of a craftsperson who works not with the mind but with the hands. A physical writing, as if words were a material substance you could still. "I worked for sixteen hours yesterday and the entirety of today, and this evening, finally, I finished the first page," he wrote about the opening of "A Simple Heart": "For half a century the women of Pont-L'Évêque envied Mme Aubain her maidservant Félicité."

Tales of such toil inspired Pound's hagiography. He admired Flaubert's dedication to finding "the word that corresponds to the thing," and the "statement that portrays, and presents, instead of making a comment, however brilliant, or an epigram." While this method of working could be understood as an anti-rhetorical realism or documentary impulse to "set down things as they are," Flaubert "execrate[d]

what is commonly called 'realism,' even though," as he wrote
to George Sand, "I'm regarded as one of its high priests." He
preferred literature to attend to a reality closer, perhaps,
to Pound's dictum that "only emotion endures." Flaubert's
"true reality" would be a "mixture of beautiful and ugly, dull
and brilliant, but in which the desire for good nevertheless
finds its place and its role." A "realism" in service to our vision of the world as shaped by devotion and belief in the
good.

Had my mother honored her own mother's wishes and remained a Catholic, my first encounter with Félicité, the
heroine of Flaubert's tale, might have been more compas-
sionate. But at the time I could ill comprehend Félicité's anx-
ious childlike faith or her devotion to Madame Aubain and
saw in them only her simplicity, which I also understood in
a snobbish and proud way as mere dim-wittedness. Neither
was I attuned to French Catholicism's unique ambiance,
even though I had lived and worked as an au pair in France
for a year when I was eighteen.

When I was "in service," neither of the families I worked
for practiced their faith, though the first produced children
so unthinkingly that, had I been taught enough about religion to form a prejudice, I might have responded to the
next pregnancy with the exclamation, "Catholics!" In both
circumstances I did have my own room, but because I was

not a *bonne,* or full-time servant, but existed in that ill-defined middle space of *au pair,* I could neither take charge of the spaces in the house traditionally given over to domestics, such as the kitchen, nor could I casually plop myself down in the living room like a family member. Under these conditions, my rooms felt more like safe houses than retreats. I was comfortable enough, but I could not leave them without a slight sense that the private family I served partly wished I hadn't. I arranged myself in the margins and, even when left totally alone, if I opened a closet or drawer elsewhere in the home, I felt that I was violating some unspoken agreement regarding what was "mine" and what was "theirs."

At my first position, my room was large and empty with wide wood-slat floors, an enormous ornate armoire, and a bookshelf filled with Harlequin Romances in French; at my second my room was small and pink and taken up almost entirely by a large comfortable bed, under which I slid the suitcase inside of which, out of some mysterious need to assure my employers that I made no presumptions regarding my longevity, I still kept most of my clothing.

"[A] cross between a chapel and a bazaar" is the way Flaubert describes Félicité's room in *A Simple Heart.* She fills it with objects of religious veneration and remembrances of the many loved ones she has lost:

On the walls there were rosaries, medals, several pictures of the Virgin, and a holy water stoup made out of a coconut. On the chest of drawers, which was draped with a cloth just like an altar, was the shell box [her nephew] had given her ... And on the nail supporting the looking glass, fastened by its ribbons, hung the little plush hat.

The hat, which she and her Mistress had found among the moth-eaten things that had belonged to Virginie, Madame Aubain's daughter who died tragically young, was typical. A sad thing with sentimental associations, thought precious for its power to conjure the memory of its former owner.

In veneration of a deceased parrot named Loulou—a late but life-changing companion in Félicité's tale—she goes a step further. She has him stuffed. After which, "[w]ith the aid of a wall-bracket, Loulou was installed on a chimney-breast that jutted out into [her] room." By this point, Félicité is old and enfeebled and extremely isolated. Her hearing and sight are failing. Each morning she wakes up to the stuffed parrot, who is "perched on a branch screwed into a mahogany base, one foot in the air, his head cocked to one side," magnificently gleaming "in the light of dawn." Some of the most critically discussed passages in Flaubert's tale follow. Seeing a colorful print of the Holy Ghost drawn in blues and reds, Félicité notices that it looks very much like Loulou. Wouldn't the ability of parrots to speak argue in favor of their kinship, over that of the dove, to that third, most mysterious member of the trinity? In the privacy of her room she prays before the print but "from time to time she would turn slightly towards the bird." Eventually Félicité goes further. She leaves off praying to the Holy Ghost—which she had always found difficult to picture, "for it was not just a bird, but a fire as well, and sometimes a breath"—and takes up "the idolatrous habit of kneeling in front of the parrot to say her prayers."

Félicité's heretical idolatry is filled with the very same innocence and pathos that endow her devotion to the ceremonies and festivals of the Catholic Church with a high serious purpose. Her contemplation of her parrot's beauty is an extension of her worship of the beauty of Christ. It is fueled by love and made possible because her faith is as simple "[as the dove] and softe," as the OED usage for "simple" records from a 1220 bestiary. The full definition reads: "Free from duplicity, dissimulation, or guile; innocent and harmless; undesigning, honest, open, straightforward." And indeed, Flaubert gives us no grounds to believe that Félicité can think two things at once. Catullus's urbane and psychologically astute "odi et amo" would be meaningless to her. Must we conclude, therefore, that there is no poetry to her? Only if we ignore Pound's distinction between the "two schools" of poetry: one simple, popular, and intelligible, the other obscure, complex, and ritualistic, "good art as the high mass is good art."

In his 1925 essay *The Religion of a Sceptic,* John Cowper Powys defends the mythopoetry of Christianity against the rational stoic who, "unable to forget a certain selfish repercussion of the feeling of moral superiority," can never know the pleasures of being emotionally swept up by a religious or aesthetic experience. "[T]he contemplation of beauty resembles the Love of Christ," he writes, which is "doubtless why it happens so often that between artists and saints there is found to be a strange and deep accord." In *The H. D. Book* Robert Duncan also locates the worship of beauty in the figures of saint and artist. Recalling reading Joyce's poetry on the lawns of Berkeley to his friends Lili and Athalie, he writes that the words on the page unlocked "some potential we felt within us." This potential, he tells us, grows in our desire to become childlike. In other words, to become simple, non-duplicitous, and to feel in an honest, open, straightforward way. What we meant by "child," Duncan specifies, "had little to do with what we had been." "It was," rather, a "secret alliance with life that we saw in artist or saint." A simple life, with the full power of your desire pointed in one direction, a life like that of Félicité, or for that matter, Flaubert.

In my twenties, curled up on a threadbare chair I had dragged in from the streets of Providence, reading *A Simple Heart* for the first time, I experienced Félicité's childlikeness as a threat. I could not abide it, trying as I was to distance myself from my own childhood and become a serious personage. Part my project of maturation was an overly energetic performance of discrimination. And that parrot threw me. It is as if Flaubert set a trap for all of us humorless bourgeois: "I know you will laugh at this, but it will prove you are heartless!"

Parrots, with their clown coloring, croaky ironic voices, head bobs, and mimicry, seem inherently comical. There is a dead-serious moment in Poe's "The Philosophy of Composition" that I've never made it past without a chuckle: "Here, then, immediately arose the idea of a non-reasoning creature capable of speech, and very naturally, a parrot, in the first instance, suggested itself, but was superseded forthwith by a Raven as equally capable of speech, and infinitely more in keeping with the intended tone." A wise rethink.

Félicité's parrot Loulou verges on the ridiculous as an object of worship precisely because his behavior while alive is so in contrast to her goodness. He beats the window panes and screeches when Madame Aubain's friends come to play cards; he laughs so loudly and unrestrainedly at the crooked solicitor, that eventually M. Bourais is forced "to creep along by the wall, hiding his face behind his hat," in order to "avoid being seen by the bird." Loulou's uncouth antics recalled those of the "imp of my autonomy," my adored pet parakeet Emile, who had only been recently killed by our cat Circe. When I read that "In [Félicité's] isolation, Loulou was almost a son or a lover to her," I must have felt a twinge of discomfort, remembering when S. had said of Emile, "he thinks you're his mate."

It's been almost thirty years since my first reading of *A Simple Heart*. Félicité's avian orisons make perfect sense to me now. Her relationship with Loulou seems healthy. It is the sentimental extremes she feels for the oblivious or undeserving humans in her life that seem ridiculous. I wince at Félicité's "outburst of frenzied grief" when forsaken by Théodore, a rogue who groped her in youth; at the "face buried in the pillow and her fists pressed against her temples" after the news reaches her that her grifter nephew has died of yellow fever. It isn't her devout and unquestioning emotional focus on one object at a time that bothers, it is her inability to discriminate. I'm like the bourgeois Madame Aubain, who cannot fathom how the servant can see no difference between her beautiful daughter Virginie and a "good-for-nothing cabin-boy."

But in youth I felt differently. Wertheresque ecstasies of emotion appealed to me, and whenever I secured a bit of solitude I indulged. But then something changed. S. agreed that we would turn the guest room of the dilapidated second-floor Providence apartment into my study. I painted the walls Wedgewood blue and snugged my Lady's Desk against the window. A room of my own in a home of my own. Unprecedented. In those confines I discovered that all the time I had longed for solitude, what I really wanted was a little privacy. The privacy to think without censure. The privacy to betray my maturity and slip back into the imaginative realms of childhood.

I lined one wall with framed versions of the fanciful dreamy paintings by children's author Cooper Edens. Some of my oldest toys—a homemade coffee-stained Humpty Dumpty, a crib doll missing a mouth—looked down upon my writing desk. I allowed my mind to embarrass me. I became ridiculous, grandiose, simple- and single-minded. I wrote poetry. "If I were to describe what goes through my mind when I write I'd be ceaselessly ridiculed and no one would ever speak to me again." That's how I explained—or didn't—what was happening in my study in my 1993 statement for *o·blēk* magazine, "Invective Verse." Though I could not bear solitude, I learned that I *needed* privacy to retrieve the lost, unselfconscious, and disinterested childhood rit-

*T*he poet Douglas Oliver had an objection. The bard had taken liberties. The crow and the rook do *not* interbreed. The crow and the rook? I'd seen a rook on the chessboard but never in a tree. Sitting straight-backed in a rumpled blue shirt and tweed blazer, Doug squinted his eyes and bid us listen: "Light thickens, and the crow / Makes wing to th' rooky wood." The lines nestled in his soft British cadence. Our thoughts took wing to consider them, but our best receptive faces failed to convince. "From *Macbeth*," he clarified. "The *crow* makes wing to the *rooky* wood." Yes, yes. But his point still eluded us. "Don't you see, the crow would *avoid* the rookery . . ." He was a fact-driven man, and as such he enjoyed offering up the things he'd long proven to himself, as both gentle test to his interlocutors and evidence of his keen observational mind. We were in the second, or maybe third hour of a dinner, and as many hours as we had sat together eating, we had drunk bottles of wine.

It was 1998. S. and I were living in Paris, spending the year's salary we'd inherited when Phyllis, his mother, suddenly, shockingly, died. She had been living alone and working as an executive secretary in Orange County when she'd formed a pulmonary embolism after flying to New Jersey to see her sister. "Economy-class syndrome," they called it. Survivable, unless the hospital to which you are admitted neglects you and you go septic. I can't remember how much money we got. Maybe $20,000, which was a lot for us at the time.

Paris that year was filled with French teenagers rollerblading over the filthy wide sidewalks, talking on clunky mobile phones. Isolated and nervous and grieving we kept mostly to ourselves. Then one day the mail brought a large envelope: a photocopied and stapled poetry magazine, not 8.5 × 11, but that awkward, European paper size, A7. The magazine, edited by Alice Notley and Douglas Oliver, was called *Gare du Nord*. It was named for Paris's "northern train station," which was just around the corner from the editors' apartment in the Tenth Arrondissement. Included with it was a hand-written note: "We hear you're in town. We'd love to have you to dinner or publish your work. Give us a call."

Douglas Oliver's pride in facts grew out of his early years working for the international press. Alice, who had only ever been a poet, didn't care about facts—at least not those defined by newspapers or lawyers or other "authoritative" sources. S. remembers one night in particular. The talk might have been of cancer or genetics or the cosmos, so topic-rich and mercurial were our dinners together, but whatever the provocation Alice suddenly banged her bird-like hand on the dinner table and insisted with steely exasperation: "I'm not made of cells!" You might have thought her genuinely angry, but her mouth moved near enough to a smile to temper any fear.

There were many such moments. In response Doug would cock his head and calmly confront her: "What are you going on about Alice? Of course you're made of cells, you see, the science of it shows . . ." he'd begin, his boyish face bright and smiling, his silver hair moistened across his forehead with the drink.

"No I'm not!" Alice would insist.

As the heated quarrel escalated S. and I would cling to our wine glasses, bleary and delighted. Doug, unable to convince her to "see reason," growing brighter and redder, would finally burst out: "Fuck you, Alice!"

"Fuck you, Doug!" she would retort.

And then they'd start to laugh in such a joyous and tender way that the seriousness of the drama would fall instantly away and S. and I, relieved, puzzled, and tight, would also laugh.

What was there to be angry about? We were eating a

tasty well-prepared meal and drinking wine in the company of great poets. Alice cooked unpretentious food that recalled my California childhood. Steamed well-seasoned broccoli, chicken, salad, bread. At Thanksgiving she went to the local butcher. He gussied up a duck *farci*, a pricey delicacy I found barely palatable, for the stuffing tasted of urinous offal when what I wanted was clear clean turkey broth and lots of celery and bread. But just to be cooked for and to be at table with an older, wiser couple was balm to us in our emotionally precarious orphaned adventure in the lonely city of lights.

Chez Alice and Doug we tested our tolerance for drink. Mornings after dinners in their addictive, warm, and frothy company we'd hazily recall stumbling down rue de Messageries to Métro Poissonnière to make our way back to the Fifteenth. "Seeing quadruple," S. would say later, which sounds fantastic but was surprisingly accurate. I can remember the sleepy four-fold street, the dumb bliss I felt reviewing the reels of provocative conversation, and that particular relief that comes from a warm human encounter with people you previously knew only in the printed pages of a book.

There's much of "sound" in what can seem true, and what can *be* true isn't always right. Despite Doug's insistence on the strictly separate spheres of crows and rooks, what were

Shakespeare's options? "Light thickens, and the <u>rook</u> / Makes wing to th' rooky wood"? Too many rooks. "Light thickens, and the crow / Makes wing to th' <u>crowy</u> wood"? "Crowy wood?" The OED has no adjective, circa 1623, for crow (no "crowy" at all), so it not only sounds bad, it was likely impossible. Crows nest in large groups made up of families, but not in colonies, called "rookeries," like rooks. An expert friend points out that Shakespeare might also have intended an echo of the word "rooky" (also "rawky" or "roky") meaning "misty or foggy," though that usage isn't written down until the end of the seventeenth century. I assert these things as though an expert, but they arise from recent, cursory knowledge. I'm far more comfortable arguing over the sound in a line of poetry than the uniquely distinct cradles of baby corvids.

It was a small thing, Doug Oliver's objection to Shakespeare's line, and I'm not sure why it remains. The year we got to know him, which none of us knew would be his last, he was at work on a long book called *Whisper 'Louise'*, which entwined his own story with that of the French radical and Communard Louise Michel. Both he and Alice were disciplined, daily writers. They arranged their small apartment with desks on facing walls, backs turned to one another. It was a model S. and I welcomed as example as we negotiated our tiny Parisian digs.

71

Associated with darkness and foreboding, in the contested Macbeth quote, the crow flies to the rooky wood at the ambiguously termed thickening "light" of twilight. But what about the rook? In Mary Webb's 1924 novel *Precious Bane*, the rook is said to have an especial sensitivity to human death. Sister and brother, Prue and Gideon Sarn, live on a remote farm in Shropshire. They have just buried their angry father. Prue goes out into the corn fields to take her brother his "nooning," or midday meal. En route she passes through the rookery—the woodsy area where the rooks roost: "I called to mind that we'd never told the rooks about a death in the place," Prue tells us. "It's an old ancient custom to tell them." The price for neglecting this inter-species bidding can be grave: "Folk say if you dunna, a discontent comes over them, and they fall into a melancholy and forget to come home . . . And though rooks do a deal of mischief, it's very unlucky to lose them, and the house they leave never has any prosperation after."

Gideon doesn't take the worry as seriously as Prue does but performs the ritual nonetheless. "Ho, rooks!" he shouts, "Father's dead, and I be maister, and I've come to say as you shall keep your housen in peace, and I'll keep ye safe from all but my own gun, and you're kindly welcome to bide." Following this ambivalent message Prue, an intuitive semiotician of Shropshire birds, tells us that, "The rooks peered down at him over their nests, and when he'd done there was a sudden clatter of wings, and they all swept up into the blue sky with a great clary, as if they were considering what was said." Up to the stars towards cosmic knowledge. "In a while they came back," Prue continues, "and settled down very serious and quiet. So we knew they meant to bide." With a laugh Gideon whets his scythe and makes utilitarian sport of the old superstition: "I'm glad they mean stopping," he says, for "I be despert fond of rooky pie."

When I read this passage, I thought of Doug Oliver. My breakfast was interrupted by a reverie over his investment in correcting this business about the "rooky wood." How was it possible that we were twenty years gone from those Parisian evenings with Alice and Doug? But then another Douglas nosed into mind causing me to doubt my memory —Douglas Rothschild. A poet friend we'd met in college, Rothschild was known for taxing a diverse company with his insistence on the falsity of Shakespeare's genius. He took Eliot's line, pronouncing *Hamlet* a failed play because it is wholly derivative and lacking an "objective correlative." I can't call to mind if he had a particular beef against *Macbeth*, but this business of conflating crows with rooks was precisely the kind of disregard for the Poundian "adequate symbol" that would have ruffled him up into the frustrated falsetto he adopted whenever making a point that nobody seemed inclined to take up. Which was often.

One thing I was sure of—Paris. And Doug and Alice's table. The complication being that there was at least one night when Douglas Rothschild dined with S. and me in that little white Tenth Arrondissement apartment filled with arresting original paintings by artists Alice had known in New York in the 1970s. Rothschild could have brought up Shakespeare's problems and prompted Doug Oliver to enter into evidence crows heading toward rook-tenanted woods. Or, I suppose it could have been possible that it was Rothschild's conundrum all alone. He does have a keen eye for nature, and birds especially. Yet still, I was all but certain that it was the older British poet who once made me mindful of the rook, so clearly did his face appear when I read Prue Sarn's account of the bird charm.

The OED calls the rook "a gregarious Eurasian crow." Its Germanic name has a similar etymology as "croak," and "probably ultimately" was an onomatopoeia for the barefaced bird's echo-throated cry. I asked S. if he remembered which Doug brought the rooks up. "No," he said. "Honestly," he went on, no scythe to sharpen but that of his tongue, "I never got all the fuss about rooks and crows, even back then." Hmmm. "Well, there are no rooks in America,"

I said . . . then I thought, but did not say, "and therefore no rookeries to tell of our dead."

Our dead. Robert Pogue Harrison writes that "the dead like to stay close to the living." Yet we, he also argues, in our restless global capitalist world of displaced people, no longer can stay close to them. When S.'s mother Phyllis discovered she was struggling to breathe, we were living on the East Coast, three thousand miles away from Orange County. Even the speed of air travel was too slow to reach a distant sickbed. His sister had called me while S. was en route with the news that Phyllis was gone. Who was there to tell? The finches around the swimming pool in the apartment complex? The gulls overhead? Some part of Phyllis's cremated body would stay in California, some part be flown back to New Jersey to lay next to her own mother. And then S. and I would distance ourselves even further from our dead, crossing the Atlantic Ocean.

We ended our Paris sojourn in June of 1999, having been abroad for eighteen months. We had spent all of our money. We had gone into debt. The good company and meals we shared with Doug and Alice during that year had been a healing balm. What a blow it was to learn, so soon after we'd returned to the States, that Doug has been diagnosed with advanced prostate cancer.

The thought recalls another vivid memory. April in

75

Paris. The song notwithstanding, it was still cold, and the sky was gray and brooding with clouds. S. and I, in the company of Alice and Doug, were trying to cross the large intersection where Blvd. Montparnasse meets Rue de Rennes. It's difficult to do by foot. The tour Montparnasse loomed above us. We were probably leaving a poetry reading, heading to a café. Completely unmindful of the threat of traffic, Doug suddenly stopped in the middle of the intersection and gazed up at the sky with joy. "The swifts!" he exclaimed, gesturing with a sweep of arm: "They've come back from Africa! Spring is here!" We all looked up to see a swoop of dark crescents high overhead. A bird sign amidst the bustling boulevard. Doug's mention of "Africa" infused the gray afternoon with the promise of sunlight. How impossible in that moment to imagine that by next year's migration he, like Phyllis, would be gone to earth.

*I*t took me a long time to admit to myself that my mom was not a good cook. Her daily fare was hampered by a fondness for short-cut or "magic" recipes that promised to produce spectacular results with little effort, evidenced by the number of dishes such as "Impossible Pie" or "Miracle Tuna" in her recipe collection. She was bored to death by the daily culinary duties and viewed hours in the kitchen as oppressive.

But there were vivid exceptions. They always took the form of elaborate cooking projects more akin to the sensual pleasures of artmaking than the drudgery of domestic service. It was as if a sort of non-utilitarian "food for food's sake" compulsion would suddenly overtake her. These projects inevitably had a cultural education angle that necessitated enlisting me, my brothers, and any neighborhood kids that happened to be hanging around.

In the fall of 1973, it was croissants. She had fallen in love with the flakey French breakfast bread the previous summer while camping in France. Every morning a freshly stocked boulangerie cart would visit the campsites. My mom would hand me a few francs and send me off with a well-rehearsed phrase, "Cinq croissants, s'il vous plait." I was nine and already quite aware of my love for warm, fresh, bready foods and anything with a high fat content. When we returned to the States, Pillsbury crescent rolls, which was what was available at the Safeway supermarket, had their weird kind of processed-food charm, but tasted nothing like the real thing. So of a weekend my mom decided that we would tackle our craving by learning to make croissants from scratch.

The green linoleum table in the breakfast room was cleared of its piles of bills and phone books to provide a large, flat surface. Here, with flour, rolling pin, and a sort of loose assembly line of tasks for us kids involving flour supply and the delivery of moist towels to keep the pastry from drying out, my mom demonstrated and supervised the delicate labor of rolling out what felt like infinite layers of thin dough and sweet butter. Squares of dough were rolled into little ziggurat mounds. The ends were crabbed inward, then placed on a sheet pan, and into the oven they went. What emerged were crispy, chestnut-brown croissants with soft, warm, airy insides. Each bite conjured a memory of those dewy mornings in frosty French campgrounds, weak

lieve that she had ever been in mortal peril. But she had. Downed, one wing dragging, I had discovered her flailing on the rough pebbly concrete of Robinson Mews—the little alleyway behind our house. A gray vulnerability by the back gate. I kneeled down beside her in my purple Sears' Toughskin™ jeans. When she did not startle or move, I knew she was wounded. I scooped her up and brought her into the house. After a ritual hydrogen-peroxide rub down, from the worry I had touched something diseased, my mother accepted my decision to rescue the pigeon. Though her rural childhood might have inured her to creature suffering, the opposite was true. She had never fully recovered from her El Paso childhood where kittens were casually drowned and decapitated chickens ran amok. Together we did triage on the bird and determined that she had a broken wing.

"The Rock Pigeon (also known as the Rock Dove) is the common pigeon seen in almost every urban area across the continent," I read in *Birds of Virginia,* surprised that a specialized regional guide would even bother to include pigeons. But I'm glad that it has, because I also learn for the first time, some forty-four years after I saved one sickly specimen of this often-maligned bird, that pigeons were "introduced from Europe, where they inhabited rocky cliffs." Modern cities are perfect for them. Who among urban dwellers has not waded through scores of pigeons in city parks? Many appear disabled, this one with a club foot, that one with missing tail feathers, another one missing an eye. The pink, fleshy legs always the most vulnerable. Despite our attempts to discourage pigeons from settling, they do not seem to fear us, cooing and courting in the public square. Whenever I see that cross-hatch of thin metal spikes outside a hotel window in Manhattan, or on a rooftop, my skin tightens. I imagine pigeon impact and cringe. Do they learn to recognize these dangers and avoid them? The damaged feet say no. I've heard people call them "flying rats," associating them with vermin and pestilence, but they are no worse vectors than ourselves. Perhaps we humans have transferred our own worries about the healthfulness of urban environments onto these concrete-and-metal colored birds from the Family *Columbidae.* A pigeon, it turns out, is really just a jaded and adaptable dove.

My mom helped me find my pigeon a temporary sick bed: a shoebox lined with a scrap of old dish towel. I provided water and a few crumbs of bread. My mother helped me to set the wing with a tongue depressor and gauze. The pigeon was small and seemed, to my ten-year-old eyes, grateful. I brought the box in the bedroom I shared with my brother Fred. I have no memory of how I kept the cats, who may have been the source of the bird's injury, away. Rooms in our house were rarely closed, but I must have arranged for a measure of caution, because my pigeon remained safe. Over the weeks of nursing her I grew fond of her gentle company, her little gray head, her reddish eyes. For the first few weeks she showed no desire to leave her shoebox, but by the time we were picking apricots, something had changed.

She began to rise and puff up her chest, as if she were trying to tell me that she was getting ready for flight. Though the gauze had been off for a week or so, she still held her wing close to her side. My mother's apricot jam project provided a perfect opportunity for a supervised reintroduction to the outdoors. I carried my pigeon's box out to the apricot tree, climbed up the step stool, and tilted the box toward a low branch. She hesitated. "It's okay," I said. "You can do it." I tipped the box slightly and she slid down and onto the branch. "You need some fresh air," I scolded her in that bossy tone children use when parenting toys and pets. When I stepped back down to the ground, my pigeon was above me looking down. She stood still on the branch and seemed nervous to be without the safety of her temporary little room. The July weather was warm and pleasant. I picked up the colander and climbed back on the step stool. We stood shoulder to shoulder, my pigeon and I, as I picked all the fuzzy, oval apricots within my reach.

At the end of the day my quiet companion willingly returned to her shoebox. And so it went for several days as the apricot project progressed. When there was no more fruit to harvest, I still made a practice of taking my pigeon out for a branch sit. In the kitchen, heaps of apricots were being skinned and sugared, boiled and cooled, an infantry of canning jars gradually filled and sealed.

A few days after the canning was completed, my mother made fresh white bread from scratch. It had the slightly sweet taste of Carnation instant milk and smelled strongly of yeast. She spread the still warm slices with butter followed by a smear of the apricot preserves we had all made together. I walked out to the backyard in my bare feet holding a thick slice in my hand. My pigeon was sitting on the apricot tree just where I had left her. My eye followed a lizard scurrying into the grass. There was a sudden sensation of upward motion and, like a shameless thought, my pigeon was gone.

*W*hen the water nymph Galatea is reunited with her shepherd lover in Handel's 1718 "pastoral entertainment" *Acis and Galatea,* she compares her joy to that of a pigeon. Using a heroic, and, according to one scholar, "unfinished" simile, Galatea sings: "As when the Dove / Laments her Love / All on the naked Spray; / When he returns, / No more she mourns." Her joyful aria of erotic reunion is preceded by a stern scolding to the "sweet youth" for whom—as John Dryden's version of the Ovid source has it—a "doubtful down" has only just begun "to shade his chin." The nereid speaks familiarly to her boy lover: "Oh, dids't thou know the Pains of absent Love, / Acis would ne'er from Galatea rove."

Galatea inhabits her desire as would the dove to which she compares herself—or so ornithologist Richard Prum would have us believe. She, like most female birds, is the "active agent" in the erotic game and chooses her mate not for his "fitness" but for his beauty. In his book *The Evolution of*

Beauty, Prum defends Darwin's hypothesis of *sexual selection*, which holds that "female sexual autonomy—the taste for the beautiful—is an independent and transformative evolutionary force." Of course, Galatea is an immortal creature and Acis a human teenager, which complicates things, as does the idealized sexuality of the pastoral landscape they inhabit. But for the mythic bucolic lovers, as for the contemporary scientist, birds are key. The "pains" of Galatea's "fierce desire" are awakened by the "thrilling strains" of spring birdsong, a "pretty warbling Quire" musically mimicked in Handel's score by the recorder. Following the *da capo* conventions of baroque opera, the heroine's repeated attempts to "hush" the warblers—and calm her own desires —are to no avail. Neither will the young Acis's yearnings be quelled, even should sheep need tending. Despite a warning by his fellow shepherd Damon about "running to thy Ruin," Acis leaves his sheep to stray in "yonder Valley" while he chases the pleasures of "billing," "cooing," "panting," and "wooing" with the lovely nereid.

John Gay is the ostensible author of the *Acis and Galatea* libretto, but barring the weary champion of the poet who bemoans "the scholarly habit of attributing, wherever possible, Gay's works to one of his more celebrated colleagues," most agree Alexander Pope and John Hughes also contributed verses to the final version. Other sources were Dryden's translation of Ovid's *Metamorphoses*—where the brief tale of Acis, Polyphemus, and Galatea appears in Book XIII —and Pope's translation of Homer's *Iliad.* My quest to uncover *which* words are Gay's, which Pope's, and which Hughes's, was only partially successful, buffeting me between the charms of speculation and the comfort of surety, but never with any conclusive result.

One source cited Pope's *Pastorals* of 1709 as contributing lines. Yet however plumped with bucolic motifs and moves similar to those that would appear in *Acis and Galatea*, no turn of phrase is shared between the two works. It is delightful to discover, however, that Pope was only sixteen years of age when he wrote his *Pastorals,* exactly the age Ovid gives to the shepherd Acis. And like the ill-fated swain, young Pope was hardly robust of frame. In the 1713– 15 Charles Jervas portrait, where the diminutive Georgian poet sits in blue satin costume and flowing wig beneath a looming bust of Homer, his beauty is so feminine one questions whether even a "doubtful down" had ever darkened his milk-white chin.

Though Pope's *Pastorals* do not match Gay's libretto, the tenets laid out in his "Discourse on Pastoral Poetry"—also written "at sixteen years of age"— reach a kind of apotheosis in *Acis and Galatea*. We should not "describe our shepherds as shepherds at this day really are," Pope asserts, but rather with "some illusion to render a Pastoral delightful," with "simplicity, brevity, and delicacy." His thinking was influenced by Frenchman René Rapin's *De Carmine Pastorali*, which attributes the very origins of poetry to shepherds imitating birdsong: "it ought to be understood of Poetry in general, so especially of *Pastoral*, which . . . was the most antient kind of Poetry, and resulting from the most *antient* way of Liveing: *Singing first began amongst Sheapards as they fed their Flocks, either by the impulse of nature, or in imitation of the notes of Birds, or the whispering of Trees.*"

And so we see what is at stake when Pope describes the muse of his *Pastorals* as so skilled as to provoke the accolades of even our original song masters, so that, "And all th'Aerial Audience clap their Wings." "Audience" is a fitting word for *Acis and Galatea* as well, for throughout this "pastoral entertainment" the fate of the bucolic lovers is witnessed, cheered, and empathized with by the natural world. One scholar charmingly calls this pathetic fallacy the shepherd's catalog of "entitlements": "For us the Zephyrs blow / For us distils the Dew; / For us unfolds the Rose, / And flow'rs display their Hue." Thus when Galetea sings "As when the Dove / Laments her Love / All on the naked Spray; / When he returns, / No more she mourns," the closing of the metaphor, her "so too do I," is implicit in the genre. The wintery picture of a "naked Spray" coyly blooms in the erotic double entendre, leading nicely to the aria's closing line: "But Loves the live-long Day." These doves take their love-making seriously.

"Happy We," sing Acis and Galatea once reunited. "Of all Youths, thou dearest Boy," sings Galatea, "Of all nymphs, thou brightest fair," sings Acis. "[T]he most refined beauty may serve as a sexual charm, and for no other purpose," wrote Darwin. An assertion Prum brings forth in service to his argument for capricious sexual mate choice based on aesthetics. But "When Beauty happens, costs will happen too," he admits, referring to the evolutionary risks of expending energy for aesthetic reasons alone. Kind of like using circuitous lyric poetry as a means of seduction. The beauty of Acis and Galatea's bucolic romance also exacts a cost, one that arises from a much more human problem: if it be proved that beauty wins out, what do we do with the beast?

The enduring nature of this dilemma came up one night when S.—while folding the week's laundry—suggested that *Acis and Galatea* was a sort of primer on sexual harassment. Ronan Farrow's article detailing the film producer Harvey Weinstein's sexual abuse and bullying of dozens of actresses had just been published and there was talk everywhere of "bad behavior" by powerful men. I laughed. But there was something to what he was saying. The Weinstein figure in

Acis and Galatea's story is the monster Polyphemus, who shows up enflamed with love for the nymph immediately following the lovers' "Happy We" reunion aria. "I rage, I melt, I burn," the one-eyed Polyphemus sings in a deep intimidating bass. In Ovid's original there's a kind of humor to the ugly monster's love-sickness. He combs his "rugged hair" with "rakes" and "mows the stubborn stubble of his cheeks" in an effort to look comely to the nymph. In the opera the comic effect is produced by having the bass sing alone with treble flute the jaunty lines:

> O ruddier than the Cherry!
> O sweeter than the Berry!
> O nymph more bright
> Than Moonshine Night!
> Like Kidlings blithe and merry.

But just as we begin to feel sympathy for Polyphemus, he changes. He becomes enraged by Galatea's rejection. He denies her agency in desire. "The Lion calls not to his Prey," she tells him, "Nor bids the Wolf the Lambkin stay." He does not listen. He brags that he's "great as Jove" and can command all the landscape and its delectables, including Galatea, to yield: "Cease to Beauty to be suing, / Ever whining, Love disdaining / Let the brave their Aims pursuing / Still be Conqu'ring not complaining." In an earlier version, this aria finished with the lines: "Force her if she's worth enjoying / She'll forgive you when 'tis over." A vulgar turn which —though missing—helps explain why the shepherd Coridon feels compelled to intervene: "Would you gain the tender Creature, / Softly, gently, kindly treat her," he calmly sings to the rapacious monster. Like a sober companion at a frat party, Coridon tries to stop Polyphemus from raping Galatea by arguing that the sex will be hotter if she's into it: "Beauty by Constraint possessing / You enjoy but half the Blessing, / Lifeless Charms without the heart."

Acis, for his part, attempts to trade in his "charms" for "arms," as if he were a lion or a wolf. "Weak as I am," he sings, "I must engage," for "[Polyphemus's] hideous love provokes my rage." "She's not worth it, Dude!" his friend Damon says, or rather, "Consider, fond Shepherd / How fleeting's the Pleasure / That flatters our Hope / In pursuit of the Fair." As the testosterone amps up between the monster and the boy, Galatea is not consulted. But knowing the monster can easily crush Acis's delicate, Alexander Pope-like figure, she entreats her shepherd lover to back down: "Cease, O cease, thou gentle youth . . ."

Neither Coridon's counsel nor Acis's meek threats work. The juggernaut of Polyphemus's frustrated desire will not be stopped: "Torture, Fury, Rage, Despair / I cannot, cannot bear!" he shouts, ripping off a "massy Ruin" from a nearby mountain and hurling it at young Acis, killing him. Polyphemus does not then, as those of us well-versed in domestic violence narratives might expect, rape or kill Galatea. Rather, he drops from the story, as if eclipsed by the generalized mourning of the entire bucolic company. The "thrilling strains" that awakened Galatea's desire are replaced by "doleful Strains" of mourning for "gentle Acis."

One interpretation reads this tale as a mythic explanation of a volcanic explosion. But with Weinstein as Polyphemus in mind, another reading occurs: the one-eyed vulgar giant as the representation of unrestrained male sexual predation. A giant penis run amok. The ugliness, therefore, has nothing to do with Polyphemus's looks, but rather with his "hideous love." "Hideous" is a word deriving from the Old French *hideous*, meaning *horror* and *fear*. A love that frightens, rather than delights. A love that denies a woman or nymph's right, just like that of the dove, to choose with whom she shares her charms.

Is Galatea to blame for provoking Polyphemus's desire? Is she a *femme fatale*? In the love-making scene Acis, as if drugged, lies at her feet. "Love in her Eyes sits playing," he sings, "And sheds delicious Death." Is this a vision of immortality such as Keats longs for in "Bright Star," or it is a vision of oblivion? In the end Galatea, distraught that "gentle Acis is no more," performs a *deus ex machina*. Referring to Acis as

*U*pon first listening, I took the lyrebird's mimetic calisthenics to be an internet hoax. However much I wanted to believe in the existence of such a marvelous creature, the performance was just too incredible. In addition to mimicking other birds, the lyrebird imitates manmade sounds. Camera shutters. Chainsaws. Car alarms. Really? Really. At least according to a BBC nature program to which my friend Devin sent me a link, after one of his trips to Australia. I clicked and listened. I walked away incredulous. The earnestness of the messenger nagged at me. This link came from *Devin*, the very paragon of honesty! And Australia was so far away and so unknown, perhaps such wondrous birds did exist there . . .

The poetry of Robert Adamson is another Australian wonder that I was introduced to by Devin. Adamson's autobiography, *Inside Out,* chronicles his empathic passion for birds. As a young boy his bird soul was so clamorous in the seeking of companions it ran afoul of the law, fatefully shaping the events of his life. Barely out of boyhood he broke into the zoo and stole a *Ptiloris magnificus,* common name magnificent riflebird, a member of *Paradisaeidae*, in English called birds-of-paradise. This action among others led to detention, and eventually jail. But there was a happy ending. While incarcerated, Adamson discovered the reason that as a boy he was so drawn to birds that he "flapped about . . . and perched rather than sat or stood": in point of fact, he was a poet.

The glossy insert of photographs bifurcating the narrative of *Inside Out* includes the young Adamson's drawing of a male riflebird. Looking inquisitively to the right, the bird's beak arches in an elegant, thin curve, like a pair of manicure scissors. A thick collar of white drapes across his rounded chest. Tail feathers wisp away from a branch gripped by little feet. The dignity and stillness of the drawing belies this bird's ability to transform himself into a fantastic dancing fan. During courtship display the riflebird's wings unfold like giant disks; he dramatically throws back his head to the right and then to the left to reveal the flashy metallic triangle of color constituted by his neck feathers. Wings held high like the Victory of Samothrace, head swaying, his legs bob while simultaneously moving backward and forward along the branch. It's very impressive. After spending some time watching videos of birds-of-paradise dancing, I think to myself: were these birds the inspiration for Sergei Diaghilev's Ballets Russes? For Merce Cunningham's fluid ritualistic movements?

The Birds-of-Paradise Project on the website of the Cornell Lab of Ornithology translates these courtship displays into the language of a more popular human groove: Disco. A throbbing sort of *Saturday Night Fever* soundtrack and sparkly pink 70s font accompanies the site's video of the most complex of these dances, that of Carola's parotia. This bird-of-paradise's courtship has several parts, which I learn must be done in strict order if he is to be successful. The moves—which include the "court hop" and the "swaying bounce"—culminate in the multi-part "ballerina dance." The name isn't very apt, and also seems a tad emasculating given the splendid machismo of these proud male birds. Why not simply the "ballet dance"? Quibble aside, the "ballerina dance" is a wonder to behold. It has four parts, the bow, the walk, the dramatic pause, and finally the *waggle*. The waggle is the best part; wings puffed out like a great umbrella opened beneath his long neck, the bird moves his head back and forth while prancing about, seemingly *en pointe*.

I first saw it in a video from that same BBC Nature program that introduced me to the lyrebird. Though there's no Bee Gees soundtrack on that video, the narration is fanciful and anthropomorphic, the dance beautiful yet contagiously

95

comic. After watching several times, I called S. into my study to witness the wonder. He was gratifyingly dazzled.

Sometime after this I was having one of my occluded days. On such, a mysterious sadness overtakes me. I feel as if a light-blocking shade has been pulled over my mind. As S. and I have been together for thirty years, he well knows the signs, and he also knows there is nothing to do but wait it out. At the end of this particular long slow draggy day I sat in bed, my hand in a book that wasn't working. S. came in and fumbled a bit with the chaos of literature around his bedside table. Then he stood up straight and held his arms to his sides, like second position in ballet. The arms became fluid wings, moving snake-like, and the hips, in a perfect side-to-side waggle, swayed in opposition to the neck. Just like magic, S. transformed himself into a human bird-of-paradise, matching Carola's parotia move for move! In one dramatic recoil, my mind's shade lifted and a laugh overcame me. One more time I begged. *Please*!

S. has always had an alluring sense of rhythm. Before we were a couple, I would on occasion spot him dancing in San Diego nightclubs. I remember watching from the sidelines as his perfectly timed hips matched pace with the synth claps of New Order's "Blue Monday" or Gang of Four's "I Love a Man in a Uniform." Though I was smitten, I was a self-conscious and mediocre dancer. Better to watch and enjoy while sipping my beer and leaning over the club's industrial-themed pipe railings, just like a female bird-of-paradise sitting on the display branch looking down at her potential mate doing his "court hop" in the clearing.

Back then a bird-of-paradise was, as far as I knew, not a bird at all, but a plant. Ubiquitous in San Diego, these deep-green tropical landscaping darlings shot up stiff fan-like leaves from the ground intermixed with brilliant orange flowers that opened like a switch blade or, as I now see so well, a bird's beak and crest. A net of mystery clung to the appellation "bird of paradise." So unlike "rose," or "daisy" or even "morning glory." What was I to make of that "of"? And did the plant's regional success mean I was living in *paradise*? Or was it from another world, somewhere so far away that anything might be possible, somewhere like . . . Australia? This made a kind of sense, given that San Diego's multitude of mottle-barked fragrant eucalyptus trees were well known to be Southern Hemisphere transplants.

After I had left the paradisiacal region of my upbringing, but many years before S. metamorphosed into Carola's parotia, it was the bird of paradise plant that presented itself as his perfect analog. The need to match man to flower was a demand made by my poem "Three Graces." Composed sometime during the first half of the 1990s, "Three Graces" was published in my first book, *Imagination Verses*. Three

Graces, three men, three flowers. Anthony was a peonie, Paul a rose, and S. a bird of paradise, "stiff" like the plant, "beneath convictions bathed in / the erotica of energy." "[H]e of all remains the one," says the prophetical poem, for he is "jeans / and a swagger, a cigarette / on which to bank one's future." But I had to wait some twenty-odd years to discover, via the autobiography of a bird soul who grew up on the other side of the planet, that my poem's use of the word "swagger," so close to *waggle,* barely concealed the fact that my lover's true analog was not the plant, but the bird it was named for.

*W*as that a member of Jacques Derrida's colloquium being eaten with relish at my feet? Or had I finally drunk too much wine? I was sitting at the corner of a long farm table with my back to open glass doors that gave onto a large grassy field. Disturbed by an unholy crunching sound, my eyes dropped from my dinner plate to the foot of my chair. There beside my sandaled foot was the farm's tomcat, the feathers of a dead grackle-sized bird splayed out beneath his head like a halo. Being a French cat—or at the very least, a *cat in France*, as I was a poet in France—he was having his dinner at the appropriate time and at table. Despite having lived my life in the company of cats, I had never before seen one eat a bird. Tom did not pluck, dress, or truss. He bit and gnawed, swallowed, and digested, "beak to tail," feathers and all. I was both mortified and fascinated. My Bordeaux hosts and their French guests were amused when I alerted them, in a tone of concern, that a cat was casually eating a whole bird at my feet.

I recall another instance of my "American supermarket

naiveté." France had a way of poking a hole in it. 1973. At nine years of age I am given a taste of warm milk fresh from a cow on a farm in the Loire Valley. My family was camped there for the night and the large frightening farmer brought my brothers and me this special treat. Having grown up on Carnation pasteurized, we couldn't palate it. This amused my mother, a one-time farm girl herself, to no end. Though I rarely questioned her omniscience, her insistence that this warm grassy beverage was superior to the chilled, white, watery 2% product to which we were accustomed was difficult to square.

Now in my early thirties I was the guest of poet Emmanuel Hocquard and artist/translator Juliette Valéry, lodgers on painter Alexandre Delay's small farm located in the Bordeaux region of France. S. and I had been invited to stay a week. The stated purpose was the completion and polishing of a French version of my serial poem "Enlightenment Evidence," the group translation of which had begun during a magical residency at the Fondation Royaumont earlier that summer. In Delay's home S. and I were given a spare, clean, second-floor bedroom with crisp linen sheets and a window overlooking the grassy field. There was a large, sunny bathroom and a small separate water closet at the end of the hall. Several of Delay's art students from Dijon were also in residence: young beautiful French people with good manners and radical ideas. On the night that tom-cat joined the feast, they had prepared the meal: a vegetarian pasta, which may have accounted for kitty's decision to fend for himself. It was nearing the end of the week and everyone felt, as people do when brought together in a temporary yet exceedingly pleasurable living arrangement, an especial fondness for each other. We drank so much red wine our teeth were stained pink.

Jacques Derrida's colloquium was held every evening at dusk, precisely when S. and I would sit down with Juliette and Emmanuel in the cool air at a round table to drink white Bordeaux and delicately peel hard-boiled quail eggs to eat with our *apéritif*. Separating Delay's property on one side was a stand of gigantic trees that wove together into what appeared to be a great hedge. It must have been at least forty-five feet high. As we sat and sipped and waited for dinner this hedge would fill with birds. Starlings, perhaps. A great racket would ensue. The din of hundreds, maybe thousands of birds. "C'est le colloque de Derrida," Emmanuel would say, gesturing in the direction of the hedge with his head. Each night on cue they'd come together to argue, this Bordeaux conference of the birds. Their colloquy well-nigh drowned out our badinage, but because of the density of the foliage, we never saw the distinct outline of a single one of these voluble debaters.

There were also three chickens. Often clustered at the edge of the property next to a small fish-filled pond constructed sometime in the past by Emmanuel, these seemingly hysterical hens would bolt toward the cocktail table looking for handouts. Clucking excitedly all the way, their puffy bodies wobbled precariously above their thin legs. Did I give a bite of quail egg to a chicken? I hope not. I was fond of these three squabbling hens, but as S. remembers it, I was much more preoccupied by the farm's billy goat, who would climb atop the chicken coop to survey his realm. Of the goat I merely recall a lesson in "tail semiotics" solemnly given me by Alexandre Delay: straight up and the goat is happy and alert; down means worried, angry, or fearful; a tail moving slowly side-to-side means the goat is in a state of contemplation, attempting to make up his mind.

Playful poets taking potshots at post-structuralist philosophers: perhaps not part of the rules of the game, but it fed our spirits well. Each day we feasted, drank, translated. One lunch we all gathered in the kitchen so that we could follow the Tour de France on the radio. "Ça a le gout du frigo," Emmanuel said, rejecting the butter at hand. It tasted as if it has been taken out and put back into the fridge over and over again. Fresh butter procured, we spread copious amounts on baguette and topped it with delicious greasy rounds of *saucisson sec*. There was cantaloupe too, and the lovely dirt-rich house wine, filled in reusable bottles by area vineyards the way we'd put out the used bottles for the Carnation milkman when I was little. Through the wide-open door of the kitchen I could see the interlocked rings of the farm's large metal bottle rack, a commonplace French object which I'd only ever seen in a Duchamp exhibit.

The tomcat, siding with the poets, finished off the philosopher's bird. I went back to my vegetarian pasta. I was trying to grok why the Dijon art students kept referring to their "potlatch," a term that interrupted their French articulations like a fish bone in the mouth. Apparently, they borrowed the idea of the Native American festival as a frame for some sort of spontaneous and collaborative artmaking. Hmmm, I thought, I wonder which Native term was shaped into that strange word, "potlatch," so like "pot luck," or, for that matter . . . pot shot. Shooting the bird outside the spirit of the hunt *merely to put in a pot and eat!* Crunch, crunch. I had learned quickly the meaning of that sound. I looked down. I should, I think, feel honored. Tom has brought me yet another member of Derrida's colloquium, whom he is presently and with great relish settling into the fixed meaning of his maw.

*I*n bird guise, the ancient Egyptian god Thoth has the head of an African sacred ibis. His slim male form ends dramatically in a sharply curved scythe-like beak. His hair is a stylized helmet of feathers. He knows many secrets: the meaning of death, the mystery of writing. As H. D. puts it, "remember, it was Thoth / with a feather // who weighed the souls / of the dead." Though the ibis evokes privileged wisdom and things hieratic, my first association with the word was mundane, common, and comfortable. A blacktop-and-bicycle feeling. It conjured the pocket-sized freedom and magical inventiveness we experience when childhood's desires metamorphose into young-adult Eros. We tug at the tether of the parental home, stretching it nigh unto breaking.

You see, when I was a girl, "ibis" was not the name of a sacred bird, but of a street. A street located at the lip of the Mission Hills neighborhood of San Diego, just west of Hillcrest, where I grew up. About ten minutes by ten-speed. On the corner of Ibis and Ft. Stockton there was a small grocery made of white stucco with an Art Deco façade called the Ibis

Market. It was a good place to stop for candy or gum. And it was only one block from Jackdaw Street. A jackdaw is a kind of small crow, but when I was standing high on the pedals of my old, battered yellow bike, pulling up on the hi-rise handlebars to lift the front tire off the ground, turning in circles, coasting, watching, Jackdaw was not a bird at all, but the name of a sleepy little street where a humble bungalow housed a boy named John Brockley, his very old mother, and his chihuahua Olivia. I, along with most of the seventh-grade class of Roosevelt Junior High School—girls and boys alike—had a crush on John Brockley. He was very tall and slim and had taut pink skin and a strong nose. He could sketch cartoons and was funny in a way that made you laugh, even when you suspected yourself the butt of his jokes. Desire infused the word "Jackdaw" with the subterfuge of surrender. I would ride past John Brockley's bungalow hoping I might be—though I hadn't the faintest idea how it might come about—undone.

Alphabetically ordered, these bird-named cross streets were the railroad ties that linked my bedroom to the untapped acquisitive desires hidden behind the doors of other people's homes. A migratory route to a newfound breeding ground that began with the Albatross and ran out at the Lark. Before hitting Hawk, Ibis, Jackdaw and Kite, there was Brant, Curlew, Dove, Eagle, Falcon, and Goldfinch.

Most of these birds are not native to the region. But even had they been, would I have paid it any mind, blinded as I was by the mating instinct? Unaware of the slew of misfortunes that would hurtle toward me in years ahead, I did not appreciate that Albatross—the street on which I lived, first in one house, and then in another, from the age of five until eighteen—was the name of a bird of great literary and mythic import. And to my young self, "Curlew" conjured not the image of a sleek shorebird with a curved beak, but a perilously steep, snake-like road that dipped down from Robinson Street into the basin of Reynard Way, which eventually led to the sea. Curlew street *curled*. It was a hazardous gauntlet down, and an arduous, almost impossible climb back. Halfway down Curlew, a right turn onto the even steeper W. Pennsylvania led down to the canyon of Dove Street.

When I was very little, we sometimes went to Dove Street to visit the Beers. They were friends of my parents and had a daughter my older brother's age named Linda. Their house was unlike any I'd ever been in: contemporary, with a large rectangular pool of tranquil water over smooth rocks in the living room and a mezzanine all around leading into the bath- and bedrooms. Their house did not smell like carpet and yeast, but rather of concrete and ginger. There was another, even steeper climb out of Dove at its northern end, leading up to the Safeway supermarket. When I was an adolescent, Dove Street was home to rough characters. A bad girl named Anita who smoked, had acne, and made out with boys. Another territory, a different gang. That this notorious street was named for a symbol of peace was wholly inoperative on the day I came home from hanging out with the Dove Street toughs. Attempting to emulate the Wilson sisters from the band Heart, I had put on my embroidered jeans and a black halter top printed with red roses. A solid half-moon of powdery dark blue shadowed my blush-colored eyelids. "You look like a prostitute," my mom said, her voice shaking as she slammed down the Bisquick. The accusation was so out of character that I have never forgotten it.

Though hardly "down the length of two continents"—which is how Fred Bodsworth describes the Eskimo curlew's migratory journey in *Last of the Curlews*—as a girl on a bike the decision to head down Curlew to Dove streets was not taken lightly, for the journey back was arduous. Often it defeated me into dismounting and walking my bike the remainder. Nobody wanted that paper route. According to Bodsworth, the migratory curlew doesn't make a decision, he only knows that "once again an irresistible inner force was pressing him to move." Yet Bodsworth allows that "even the curlew's simple brain sensed vaguely" that his migratory journey "was a long, grim gantlet of storm, foe and death." Was this the same vague sense of doom I had when Anita took me to the flat of an older hippie whom she asserted would give us pot? He was unkempt but weirdly proprietary, clamping his arm around her neck.

At the end of Albatross Street there was a rudimentary roundabout marked by a central ring of shrubbery. It gave egress onto another steep branch of W. Pennsylvania off of which Brant spoked to the left. Brant was a small street that dead-ended in a canyon where my friend Tracy lived in a large white Spanish-style house. "Brant" is a word that doesn't sound like a bird, but is. A small goose with a black neck and a white collar, migratory like the curlew. Though Tracy and her brother outnumbered their single mother by one, their house never felt like a place where kids lived. The interior was dramatically decorated and spare. In it I felt wary that I might be confronted by something I was not prepared for. This perilous adult ambiance leant edge to the game of spin-the-bottle we played one night in the sequestered basement bedroom of Tracy's brother Scott. Afterwards, I floated home in the dark, the residual touch of Jim Lapp's lips having changed the feel of my own.

"For it was a blessing of their rudimentary brains that they couldn't see themselves in the stark perspective of reality," Bodsworth writes of the curlew's ignorance of the perils involved in its migration. Nor does the adolescent brain—to the chagrin of parents—care to register the "stark perspective of reality" that is pregnancy, venereal disease, heartbreak. But what greater heartbreak than preparing for the mate that never comes? That is the narrative around which the ecological pathos of *Last of the Curlews* circles. It tells the story of a male Eskimo curlew who is, seemingly, the last of his kind. As the story begins, we watch the curlew as he secures and defends an arctic territory in the hopes of luring a female. He flies concentrically above his ground and projects his desperate mating song, but no female comes.

"The Fountain," a poem which appeared in my 2009 book *Clampdown,* recounts the restless outdoor quest Eros compelled in me when a teen. "As a girl / I cruised like a boy," I wrote, "in daylight and / open-air spaces." An earlier draft lacked "in daylight," but it is an important detail. Curfews meant covert twelve-year-old gropes took place under bright sunlight. When John Brockley finally yielded, I had a bad cold. We walked down the pebbly alleyway behind my house holding hands. We paused against a garage. I opened my mouth and allowed his tongue in.

When the Eskimo curlew finds a lone female on the northern leg of his migratory journey, he proffers her a snail. Taking the mollusk in her beak seals their bond. Though I let John and others kiss me freely, there was no magic key nor ritual offering assuring their return. The curlews will not be parted except by a bullet. They are the last of their species because they were shot down by the hundreds in the nineteenth century, trusting and fleet and fearing no predator. I had plenty of willing mates. Yet every opportunity felt precarious and desperate. As "The Fountain" has it, regret grows from the kiss unstolen, the flesh uncaressed, the loneliness unabated. The poem culminates in a night spent suffering "passively" in a sleeping bag next to a boy I desired. Coyness, as Marvell knew, is a crime that colludes with patience, and it is no friend of youth.

Birds court, but are they coy? The male Eskimo curlew stops often before the female to "strut like a game cock . . . with his throat puffed out and tall feathers expanded into a great fan over his back." The female responds, "by crouching, her wings aquiver," begging for food "like a young bird." The male offers nourishment and their beaks touch. Our lips are soft and moist, while beaks are hard and dry. Yet many birds' lovemaking includes something that looks like kissing: face to face, beaks scissoring and clacking. Albatross touch their beaks together in a gesture that resembles sword play, but of a sweet, syncopated nature. It is cheering to look upon. The meaning of "cheer"—I learn from an Ann Lauterbach poem—was once "'the face, the countenance,' especially as expressing emotion." Do I anthropomorphize by referring to bird countenances, kissing beaks?

The albatross is endangered, the ibis is making a tentative comeback, but the Eskimo curlew is gone. There have been a few sightings of lone specimens, but they are unconfirmed and perhaps wishful. The bird-named streets of my childhood remain, though the friends they housed have long ago left. I would hazard that a similar ragtag group of horny teens has taken our place, but these San Diego neighborhoods have become so expensive that I doubt such as us could live there again. Single mothers like Tracy's or John Brockley's could not afford the quaint bungalows on Jackdaw, Ibis, Curlew, or Brant as they could in the nineteen-seventies. And Albatross Street, once rather unkempt and overgrown, feels opulent and closed. One definition of "growing up," claims "The Fountain," is "learning / to loathe what's cheap / and what's free." On those bird streets the possibility of Eros was free, if somehow still just out of reach. But compared with real impossibility, a missed opportunity is a feeble tragedy. How would I have borne my baffling hunger had I ridden my bike along those bird streets vaguely sensing that there were no boys left in all the known world?

*M*y mother will soon be dead. I know this, and I do not. So fierce is she that I have come to think of her as a distinct species, exempt from our common share in morbidity. Or perhaps this is merely a wish. It is February 1989. In an unprecedented détente, I am not speaking to this all-powerful creature from whom, it is said, I issued. During one of my daily visits to check on the needs of her cancer-ridden body she, quite out of character, and without warning or provocation, had burst into a rage and begun to berate me. I turned my back on her and left. Then I bloomed with a sickly guilt... *I dread that she will cast me away, / for I fall, I mis-take, I fail in her mission.*

A few weeks later S., in our new nightly poem-reading ritual, chooses Robert Duncan's "My Mother Would Be a Falconress." I lie on our bed during his recitation, paralyzed by self-reproach. The strange hypnotic cadence, the medieval mood, the high poetic tone, the alluring use of the strange conditional "would be," the mysterious word "gerfalcon," the controlling, yet caring falconress riding with her "gay falcon" on her wrist—all of it gets to me. But it is the shame of recognition that undoes me: *She uses a barb that brings me to cower.* It does not matter as I listen that I know nothing of falconry: *For she has muffled my dreams in the hood she has made me, / sewn round with bells, jangling when I move.*

"Throughout history powerful women have practiced falconry—from Russian tsarinas and English queens to Bavarian noblewomen," I read in an article on falconry in the October 2018 issue of *National Geographic.* I am now in my fifties. My mother has been dead for almost thirty years. At long last I learn that gyrfalcons (not "gerfalcon" as it is spelled in the poem) are the largest of the falcon species and "highly intelligent." They were "introduced to European falconers by Norse merchants and became Iceland's most precious export during the Middle Ages." The article includes a beautiful painting of a medieval noblewoman with an arctic gyr sitting on her gloved wrist. She is blonde and pale, childlike and caring. Her head is bent toward the bird, her lips poised as if she's cooing. Looking closely I can see that her gloved hand holds not only the bird but a golden cord wrapped like a lasso. This is the "creance": "a long fine line or cord attached to a hawk's leash, by which she is restrained from flying away when being trained" (OED). The name of

to me that I'd have a girl," my tomboy mother liked to say, as if she were still sorting out how the mix-up came about.

In the preface to my first book of poems I would write: "Where literature is found has less to do with its force than who we are when we find it." When my ears took in Duncan's "My Mother Would Be a Falconress" for the first time, I was a young woman who one minute was longing to fly *far, far beyond the curb* of my mother's will, and the very next wishing that my mother and I would never be parted:

> Yet it would have been beautiful, if she would have
>   carried me,
> always, in a little hood with the bells ringing,
> at her wrist, and her riding
> to the great falcon hunt, and me
> flying up to the curb of my heart from her heart . . .

I was these things and the poem knew it. It knew that I could love, fear, and even—though I could hardly admit it— *hate* my mother. It knew the power of psychological captivity. It knew what it was like to feel disoriented in an emotional labyrinth through which the only thread that can guide you out is held by the hand that entrapped you.

Not remotely strong enough to break from my mother's creance, I had, unconsciously, found one of my own species to help me by falling in love with S. That my first steps toward an adult relationship might put my dream of being *carried . . . always* by my mother in serious jeopardy never occurred to me. I had forgotten a central, though never explicitly articulated, rule of my training: *She draws a limit to my flight. / Never beyond my sight, she says.* My mother's jealousy was always couched as concern: "I only wish," she said to me a few weeks after we'd ended our détente, "considering you now have *conflicting loyalties*, that I didn't have to burden you with my illness . . ."

I heard and I read "My Mother Would Be a Falconress" as a poem, paying no heed to "A Lammas Tiding," the prose piece that precedes it in Duncan's 1968 volume *Bending the Bow* and that serves to explain its genesis. Had I done so, I would have learned that, in falconry, hoods are not, in fact, "sewn round with little bells," a detail which had always struck me as particularly cruel but which I took on faith as accurate. I had long been disquieted by the fact that things may enter our ears against our will. As a girl, even the noise from my heartbeat, as it bounced off my pillow, frightened me. Would it never stop? . . . *where I dream in my little hood with many bells / jangling, when I'd turn my head.*

To me those bells sewn round the hood were an allegory for the superego's complicity with the mother's voice, jangling with every move of the head. The poem speaks of a *hooded silence* that leads to sleep, but it has been my experience that, even in sleep, the bells keep ringing. They peal through the portal of dreams. That is why, I tell myself, my dreamlife often seems wholly ignorant of the waking fact that my mother is dead.

The poem also knows that death is not the end of it:

> My mother would be a falconress,
> and even now, years after this,
> when the wounds I left her had surely heald,
> and the woman is dead,
> her fierce eyes closed, and if her heart
> were broken, it is stilld   •
>
> I would be a falcon and go free.
> I tread her wrist and wear the hood,
> talking to myself, and would draw blood.

This denouement follows a climax in which, in his attempt to reach the nesting ground of the other falcons, the bird/child in the poem defies the falconress/mother by flying "high, high in the air." In mythic fashion he looks "west to the dying sun," where, he says poignantly: "it seemd my human soul went down in flames." The human soul goes down so that the bird soul may soar.

But what would it mean for a poet's avian soul to be cast in the form of a falcon rather than a songbird? Turned to killing, driven by the hunt. And what would happen if a songbird were kept and trained by a falconress who wished she were a raptor? How will the bird *fail in her mission,* though she desires what her trainer desires?

> When will she let me bring down the little birds,
> pierced from their flight with their necks broken,
> their heads like flowers limp from the stem?

To my young mind the "little birds" that the trained falcon must bring back to the falconress stood for every bit of life I sought outside of my mother's purview. Each tidbit brought back and placed before her, in compensation for the life she'd sacrificed to my training, that she might enhance her limited existence vicariously through my own:

> as if I were her own
> pride, as if her pride
> knew no limits, as if her mind
> sought in me flight beyond the horizon.

My mother's favorite "little birds," I learned one day at the age of twenty, were poems. She had wanted to be a writer, a fiction writer. I would be a writer, a poet. Each poem I brought back "perfectly" was praised: *She rewards me with meat for my dinner.* What, I wondered, would become of these little bird poems once the falconress's *fierce eyes* were closed for good?

Which leads me to ask once again: must a woman die for a poet to be born? I was twenty-five years old and had been writing poetry since the age of twenty when my mother's cancer finally claimed her life. I thought I was a poet, and in some ways I was. But grief for this woman changed me. And in the wake of her death all of the poems—those perfect little birds—became as limp as broken flowers, mere juvenilia. Had I been freed, or had I finally entered into what would become my "appalling destiny"? I was miserable and knew not who I was without my mother's commands. When death took her from me my human soul went down in flames. Now I was all bird, and had nothing left to do but sing.

*I*t is preferable to be Baudelaire's caged swan covered in dirt than Eurydice stricken; preferable to live any life as a bird than enter the world though the body of a woman. Or so Orpheus believes when, returning to Earth after a millennium in the "other world," he has his pick of souls. The frustratingly impoverished account of this fascinating decision by the Thracian singer is included by Plato in Book X of *The Republic*. Plato's signature narrative gambit of placing fantastical truths in the mouths of interlocutors at several removes is in full force in this tale, known as the "Vision of Er." Er is a soldier who dies in battle. He spends twelve days in "the other world," and then, having been designated a hermetic messenger, returns to life. Er's vision is told by Socrates to Glaucon like a disturbing bedtime story: "Once upon a time he died in war," Socrates begins. He proceeds to describe an elaborate processing center—part royal tribunal, part Las Vegas casino—at the threshold between life and death. Souls of men and animals come and go through a quartet of portals located at a "demonic place": an entry and exit to the right and up to heaven, the same on the left leading down into earth. Judges sitting between the openings hang signs of judgment around the necks of the souls of the recent dead: the holy and just are sent to the right, the evil and treacherous to the left. All the while souls who have been on a thousand-year journey in the places these openings lead to are returning to the processing center, returning to life.

This is where the Las Vegas part comes in. Before beginning "another death-bringing cycle" these souls go on a sort of cosmic camping trip to the outer reaches of the cosmos where a "certain spokesman" pulls a bunch of "life lots" out of one of the Fates' lap and scatters them like dice in front of the awaiting souls. Then each must choose their own demon . . .

Not surprisingly, many choose badly.

It is a baroque tale Socrates seems to have designed to impress upon Glaucon the importance of study and learning in order to gain the wisdom to choose "between the worse and the better life." For "if he chooses intelligently and lives earnestly, a life to content him is laid up, not a bad one."

According to Socrates, Er describes the lottery of souls as "pitiable, laughable, and wonderful to see." "For the most part," he continues, each soul chooses "according to the habituation of their former life." And here is where Orpheus comes in.

Er relates how "he saw a soul that once belonged to Orpheus choosing a life of a swan, out of hatred for womankind." The seed of Orpheus's thousand-year misogyny was the bloody *sparagmos* visited upon him by Maenads: "due to his death at their hands, he wasn't willing to be born, generated in a woman." Unlike the violence-born flesh-into-feather metamorphoses of Philomela and Procne, Orpheus gets to choose. As do nonhuman creatures in this place: Er reports having seen a swan and "other musical animals" choosing to return in human form. The song is the bond between them.

Did that same vanity that led Orpheus to believe he could defy the rules of the underworld influence his decision? Was he taken in by the Greek legend that, in the face of death, swans make, as Tennyson would centuries later describe it, "a music strange and manifold"? I shudder to think of the poet, once hatched and grown, discovering the melodic impotence of his long beautiful white neck.

The egg as a mechanism of birth conjures an illusory cleanliness: the crisp shell, the sealed efficiency, both so seemingly distinct from the fleshy uncertainty of the vaginal cavity. In the Orphic Theogony, Time forms a Cosmic Egg in Aether, which splits to release into the mist the first generation of gods. Orpheus sings a version of this story in the *Argonautica*.

As I imagine Orpheus in the guise of a swan, I struggle to push from my mind that tacky but compelling "classic rock" logo of the Swan Song label on Led Zeppelin albums: A wingèd man, knotty and muscular, back arched, arms thrown up against a red sky above what looks like a Martian landscape, head back in the ecstatic throes of death. The logo is a copy, with color added, of an 1870 drawing by American artist William Rimmer. Reminiscent of Zep's lead singer, the swan-man logo has a hyper-defined cleft chin and mane of wavy hair. His enormous wings stand out against the red backdrop, huge, white, and feathery. There is something painful about his hybrid state, the strain not of ecstasy but of wrong embodiment, as if the wings are not a means to soar but a mechanism of manipulation. And he has no genitals. The sexuality of this swan-man, like the musicality of the swan, is nonexistent.

Er sees another Thracian poet in the "other world": the lesser-known Thamyris. Legend has it that Thamyris was struck dumb by the Muses for proposing a singing contest with their maidenhead as prize. That's one story. In another he loves the tender youth called Hyacinth, a favorite of Apollo. It is said that Thamyris was the first man to love another, though Ovid mixes the tales and gives this distinction to the grieving Orpheus.

Like Orpheus, Thamyris chooses to eschew regenera-

*I*n the November 2019 issue of *Scientific American* I read that an extra germ-line-restricted chromosome has been discovered across the "family tree of songbirds." This chromosome may have enough differentiation from songbird to songbird to account for the amazing speciation that is found among birds that sing—5,000 distinct species, all possibly from a "common ancestor . . . 35 million years ago." A breakthrough in the study of songbirds, whose baffling diversification had heretofore been attributed variously to "climate change, plate tectonics and sexual selection." It all goes back to the asteroid: 66 million years ago it crashed into Earth destroying "all of the nonbird dinosaurs and most birds." The only survivors were the neornithines—feathered ancestors of the birds with whom we now share the planet. The chromosome's role in one of the "greatest evolutionary radiations of all time" isn't entirely clear, but "suggests [that] a genetic mechanism" helped to promote speciation.

How long had I heard, without qualm or need to fact-check, that birds evolved from dinosaurs? Gazing at a circling raptor, or contemplating the weirdly ancient face of a budgerigar, this lineage never struck me as farfetched. But this article complexified that hearsay ancestry. Without the demise of *most* of the dinosaurs, we might not have had song-birds at all. The smaller-brained species' extinction gave these wingèd musicians an in. If what René Rapin's *De Carmine Pastorali* claims is true, that "singing first began amongst Sheapards . . . in imitation of the notes of Birds," then we have the asteroid to thank for poetry. No asteroid, no songbirds, no songbirds, no poets, no poets, no poetry . . . But, luckily for us, that's not the way things went.

Remembering my childhood journeys into the Mesozoic —via picture books or, most dreamily, the Disneyland train ride through "Primeval World," a cavernous diorama filled with lush giant plants, circling pterodactyls, and enormous herbivores with waterfalls of roping leaves draping down from their mouths—I wonder to myself: How large were those bird ancestors, those "neo" "ornithines" anyway? What were they like? Perhaps D. H. Lawrence's Jurassic-fantasia "Humming-Bird" lends a clue. It is one of only four poems about birds in his 1923 collection *Birds, Beasts and Flowers*. The shortest one.

"I can imagine," begins the poem, "Before anything had a soul," "in some otherworld / Primeval-dumb . . . Humming-birds raced down the avenues." Lawrence describes the iridescent hummingbird—whose heart can beat over one thousand times per minute—as a "little bit" which "chipped off in brilliance" from a half-inanimate "heave of Matter," to go whizzing through "slow, vast, succulent stems."

"I believe there were no flowers," Lawrence speculates, when "the humming-bird flashed ahead of creation." Instead of syphoning nectar from petal-funnels the hummingbird pierced "vegetable veins with his long beak." Lawrence makes me see that "bit" like a glittery fleck, a darting firefly against the Mesozoic ooze. Then the poem takes a turn. With pre-CGI phanopoetic magic, the insect-like hummingbird suddenly swells to gigantic proportions: "Probably he was big / As mosses . . . / Probably he was a jabbing, terrifying monster"! As if hummingbirds *still* inhabited that primordial world, Lawrence ends his poem by claiming, "We look at [the hummingbird] through the wrong end of the long telescope of Time." And so for the poet these miraculous birds are actually hovering apertures into deep temporal pockets, and it is only our distorted view that reduces the "jabbing, terrifying monster" into a tiny speck. "Luckily for us," Lawrence, as if possessed of a secret dispatch, ends his strange little poem.

Does the temporal rift Lawrence posits between the hummingbird and us also account for the inaudibility of their songs? Yes, I discover, hummingbirds—though they belong to a distinct avian order called *Trochiliformes*—are songbirds. The wing-sound for which they are named is not their intended music. I take an internet journey to the Cornell Lab of Ornithology to listen. Hummingbird music is cutting edge: clicks, buzzes, hums, and croaks. Their songs are challenging and intricate, alluring and sometimes speech-like. The avant-garde of the deepest past.

The three other birds Lawrence deals of in *Birds, Beasts and Flowers* are also ones he encountered in America: the turkey cock, the eagle, and the blue jay. As with the hummingbird, he sees these birds with the eye of a reluctantly civilized man heading giddily back in time. Repulsed and fascinated by the turkey cock's "red hot" wattle, which he calls a "Dross-jabot," he asks, "Are you the bird of the next dawn?" Of the "acid-blue metallic" jay, who caws at him and his little black dog, he queries: "Whose boss are you, with all your bully way?"

Next to these comic portraits, the eagle elicits respect. He is a "Sun-breaster," a sword of Damocles circling in the sky. In a vivid homoerotic image, the eagle is "Erect, with the god-thrust entering him from below." Lawrence asks the noble raptor, "Why do you front the sun so obstinately . . . As if you owed him an old, old grudge, great sun: or an old, old allegiance." Is there a "bond of bloodshed" between the eagle and sun? Even if so, Lawrence grimly concludes, this magnificent blood-thirsty bird and the "sun in heaven," to which he offers his sacrifice of a "red smoky heart from a rabbit," can be put "out of office" "By the life in the hearts of men."

"Imperial Rome had subjugated a world to the law and order of its Caesars under that wingèd predator; and wherever the arrogance of world dominion goes the eagle appears on its standards," writes Robert Duncan in "Man's Fulfillment in Order and Strife." What if, instead of the bald eagle, our national bird had been the "skinny repulsive"—to use Lawrence's words— turkey cock? Benjamin Franklin, Duncan tells us, argued for such "in his domestic pride." "In our sense of how inappropriate the turkey is," Duncan notes, we "almost snicker." "[W]e can see how much our own sense of dignity has departed from that of men like Franklin and how much it demands the Mithraic imperium of the Bird of War."

What if, instead of the bald eagle or the turkey cock, we had chosen a songbird to represent our nation, had put a hummingbird upon a standard? Would the life in the hearts of men have been altered from the Mithraic imperium to a *pax poeticae*? Would the unacknowledged legislators have become presidential poets? I can't help but think that the harm would have moved in the other direction, damaging songbird and poet alike. And yet, there's one singer that just might fit the bill: that perky familial blue jay, dressed in Dallas Cowboy colors and, in all his "bully way," cacophonously cawing at the foreigner out walking his dog.

But the hummingbird? Absurd. That little primordial fleck will not be stilled into a settled sign. Luckily for us.

I am trying to relax enough to relieve my bladder. This will get easier as the evening progresses and I drink more wine, but right now, cognizant of the close-quarters company, it takes some effort. It helps to focus on things other than the task at hand. In Keith and Rosmarie Waldrop's cramped and crowded first floor "half bath," this is easy. The walls are lined with shelves filled with compact discs. I am surrounded by the American songbook, blues, and classic jazz; box sets of Louis Armstrong, Billie Holiday, Betty Carter, Django Reinhardt, and Thelonious Monk. The complete Prestige recordings of Eric Dolphy, too tall to fit, sits on the floor, leaning against a shelf, next to an old, heavy, industrial-looking paper cutter. Mid-twentieth-century office green.

What little of the gray-and-white tile wainscoting that is not obscured by recorded music is covered by those white moveable words once marketed in bookstores and gifts shops as "magnetic poetry." There must be lead in the tiles. Above the wainscoting the walls are crammed with Keith's collages. Mismatched frames of various shapes and sizes, some slightly askew. I see a paper-doll-sized colorful comic-book superhero superimposed over the giant faces of two women: Renaissance portraits or Greek goddesses? Is that Rodin's *The Kiss* in the corner of a field of milky abstraction? Some of the collages are three-dimensional: open boxes containing wood, string, and glass vessels nestled in front of pasted cutouts of colored paper and printed images.

There are upwards of fifteen original artworks on the walls of this small lavatory, a fraction of Keith's output. In the rooms where S. and I sleep when we visit, at the very top of the house, are hundreds more. Lined up like LPs against the walls, leaning this way and that on banks of grey metal shelves.

Keith loves bathroom humor. Above the toilet tank in the little half-bath is a small red sign reading "Aqua Non-Potabile." The full bath on the second floor has a broken municipal "One-Way" street sign tacked above the toilet. Pointing downward. In his section of the joint autobiography he wrote with Rosmarie, he recounts how, in their first shared home in Michigan, they shelved books in the bathroom "with something in the title or author to suggest that locus." Thus *Ubu Roi, The Golden Pot*... "Anything by Adelaide Crapsey... The Sitwells. The Brownings... *Howard's End / Gone with the Wind*," and so on. His jocoserious book

The Real Subject: Queries and Conjectures of Jacob Delafon with Sample Poems takes its hero's name from a French toilet manufacturer. Thus a man in France standing before the "john"—as Keith's generation would say—would often find himself in the company of Jacob Delafon, whose name would be printed at twelve o'clock on the pedestal. As a woman, my vista is different.

In this bathroom it is a full-sized poster of Max Ernst's collage titled *The Birdman*. Covered by a thin layer of plastic and poorly tacked to the back of the door, its edges curl inward. The poster does not fit inside the door's indented panel, but awkwardly straddles it.

I have used this bathroom more times than I can count over the past thirty years. It is my first destination when S. and I arrive chez Waldrop following the five-hour drive from our home in central Maine. Its shy-making location, right next to the dining-room table, is not ideal. We've eaten so many wonderful dinners at that table in the company of writers both famous and obscure. How many have had to excuse themselves and "use the facilities" mid-meal? Though I have no memory of it, S. was scarred by hearing a star Brown professor enter this little room in the middle of dinner and throw up. As S. tells it, following the expulsion, he rejoined the meal as if nothing had happened. I remember that evening, but not the famous semiotician's regurgitations. I was either too deep in my cups or too repressed to admit what I was actually hearing.

I imagine that it was Keith's admiration for Ernst that inspired him, however long ago, to become a collagist. To really get serious about scissors and glue. Which makes me think it quite cheeky of him to put Max the Birdman up in the bathroom. He is there to confront you when you pull the little string on the lavatory's one source of light: a 1960s frosted glass sconce, just left of the window.

But unlike Ernst's images, Keith's collages, even those representing naked women—of which there are many—are not menacing. They are playful and humorous. Some are slightly haunting. Many are tinged with melancholy. This poster of Max the Birdman is different. It is disturbing. From where I sit it gives me a deep frisson in the arch of my foot.

There is a man dressed in a loose-fitting jacket and trousers. A Victorian brigand, perhaps. He wields a knife. But in place of a swarthy bearded visage, he has the head of a bird. It could be a mask or an elaborate hood. But whether the figure is in disguise or is some sort of terrifying avian chimera is unclear enough to be truly frightening. The Birdman stands in a dynamic posture, but his head, like the falcon-headed Egyptian god Horus, is pictured in stiff profile. His bird-eye is expressive—seeming to look out at the viewer and inward at the same time—as if watching his instincts with an alien intelligence.

His knife is struck through the arch of a naked woman's smallish foot. Red seeps down her leg. I find the physics of her posture upsetting. Seen from her backside, it looks as if the Birdman is holding her aloft by this knife in the foot; though the weight of her body would make this impossible. The knife would cut through the flesh. Her face is turned away. We see only her dark hair elaborately piled atop her prone head. One of her legs bends towards her sensuous buttocks. The other is obscured or missing. One of her arms reaches toward the ground, the other lays delicately against her side. She seems to both flail and float.

At the bottom of the image the artist has written in cursive letters "Max—The Birdman—Ernst." The proper name is much larger than the epithet, though the latter is in all caps and acts like a ligature between the lowercase "max" and "ernst." It is as if Ernst is not only titling and signing this work, but presenting it as a sort of surreal self-portrait: a psychological avatar. The bird head, probably cut from an ornithologist's or naturalist's notebook, looks sinister and indifferent to the woman's plight. There's a dynamism and strangeness that enhances the threatening ambiance of the image. Layers of armor-like feathers in profile. The cruel curve of a yellowish beak. The beak echoes the knife.

The bird's feathers resemble reptile scales or metal armor, against which the softness of the woman's body looks especially vulnerable.

Though I was barely twenty when I translated Paul Éluard's poem "Max Ernst," the opening lines have stuck with me: "Dans un coin l'inceste agile / Tourne autour de la virginité d'une petite robe." I pull the typescript from my files. Trace of my old Smith Corona. I had retyped the French version, adding the accents by hand. At first I rendered the opening lines quite literally, "In a corner agile incest / Turns around the virginity of a little dress." Later, I allowed myself more leeway, "Agile incest in a corner / circling a virgin dress." I thought the image playful, even a little magical. I didn't see the dress as a synecdoche, but literally: a little girl's dress—like the one worn by Alice in John Tenniel's illustrations—hovering in a corner. Its emptiness erotic. I was an asymmetrical Freudian, imagining desire to move up from the child to the parent, but not the other way around. Now the idea of "agile incest" circling like a falcon waiting to strike seems to me rather creepy. Like something out of David Lynch's *Twin Peaks*.

In my twenties, my negative capability was impeccable. I don't recall questing after the identity behind Éluard's eponymous poem, nor did I imagined it to be an ekphrasis, which I now think probable. Even had I been curious enough to make the effort, there was no Google in 1986, and I am not sure that I would have possessed the know-how to research such questions had I been able to formulate them. But I feel quite certain that this poem—indeed, all those surrealist stanzas that I translated from Éluard's *Capitale de la douleur*—served to tune my sensibilities one key closer toward the aesthetic orchestrations I would encounter, about five years later, when I first walked into the Waldrop's home at 71 Elmgrove Avenue. The interior, up to and including every inch of the bathroom, overtaken by the collage aesthetic and surrealist imaginary. Not exclusively, but significantly. The Victorian detritus and erotic jokes, the dialogue between technologies and times: photography, paint, and print, primitivism and the avant-garde. All so European. I recognize now how Max Ernst's collage of the Birdman traffics in underworld stereotypes and arouses bourgeois fears, and that even, or perhaps especially, in the context of a cramped lavatory, it still works to disturb me, after all these years.

"*Their* wings a blur / as they streaked down from heaven / across the bright sky—"

I appreciate Stanley Lombardo's translation of these lines from Sappho 1, describing the furiously flying sparrows that pull Aphrodite's chariot down from heaven. In contradistinction to the incongruity of such tiny birds hauling the weight of such an awesome goddess, English delivers a vocalic congruence between "chariot" and "sparrow": "drove your chariot pulled by sparrows / swift and beautiful / over the black earth." Anne Carson's version describes the sparrows as "whipping their wings," but when I think of the effort such small birds would have to make in this scenario, Lombardo's word "blur" just captures it. I can only accept that—provided it's a "simple question of weight ratio"—an entire flock of sparrows, each in its own tiny harness, would be needed to pull even the daintiest of divine chariots. Yet Mary Barnard, in her free, one might even say, profligate, version, renders the lines as follows: "to your / gold car, to yoke the pair whose / beautiful thick-feathered wings // oaring down mid-air from heaven / carried you to light swiftly / on dark earth." Did she choose to leave the word "sparrow" out because she limited them to "a pair"? That way we might imagine some grander bird "oaring down" from Olympus. Richmond Lattimore's version seems more realistic. He describes the chariot-parted air as "trembling at the heart to the pulse of countless / fluttering wingbeats"!

Sappho's representation of sparrows as sacred to the goddess of love must be behind the tradition of rendering the Latin word "passer"—wherefrom descends our word for songbirds, *passerines*—as "sparrow," as seen in the most charming and flirtatious of poems from the Classical era, Catullus 2. *Passer, deliciae meae puellae*, it begins, "Sparrow, pet of my girl." In a sulky apostrophe, the lover covets his beloved's pet sparrow's place of privilege in both her heart and between her breasts (*in sinu*, ablative of *sinus*, which can mean curve, hollow, bosom, or lap).

Peter Whigham, my favorite translator of Catullus, takes the liberty of inserting the proper names "Lesbia" and "Catullus" into the poem, and of solving the multiple meanings of *sinus* by including both:

> Lesbia's sparrow!
>> Lesbia's plaything!
> in her lap or at her breast
> When Catullus's desire
>> gleams ...

>> you are invited to nip her finger
>> you are coaxed into pecking sharply

His English brings out the fetish quality of the sparrow, interaction with which stands in place of more conventional means of erotic satisfaction— "if I could play with you / her sparrow ..."

>> I should be eased
> as the girl was of her virginity ...

Whigham lineates the Latin poet's quantitative verses using William Carlos Williams's variable foot, and dedicates his translation to the memory of the American poet. "A year or so before his death," Whigham tells us in his acknowledgment, "William Carlos Williams had some of these poems read to him. He handed them around among his friends. Not only his example as a poet but this practical encouragement of his as a master was a great help to me at a time when the book might well have been left in an incomplete state ..."

Williams died in 1963, the same year in which his collection of poems *Pictures from Brueghel* was posthumously awarded the Pulitzer Prize. In the first section of this collection Williams makes explicit reference to Catullus's playful erotic emblem in his short poem, "Sappho, Be Comforted." "There is only one love," he says in his address to the Lesbian poet, "let it be a sparrow / to hold between the breasts." In "The Sparrow," however, from the *Journey to Love* section, Williams's paean to Lesbia's pet of choice drops any dainty double-entendre in favor of a robust portrait of this homely little bird, who is clearly a feathered mirror for Williams's enjoyment of his own rough-hewn appetites. Though the poem is dedicated to Williams's father, it is the spitting image of the son:

> The cockerel, the crow
>
>> with their challenging voices
>
> cannot surpass
>
>> the insistence
>
>>> of his cheep!

This is the "cheep" of the sparrow carrying on his spring "amours," the instinctual music of nature's call. It also serves as a description of Williams's poetics when contrasted to the "challenging voices" of some of his more highbrow modernist contemporaries. Williams starts his poem by insisting on the artifice of the sparrow's lusty cry: it is a "trait / more related to music / than otherwise"; "a poetic truth / more than a natural one." Unlike the lines which end his poem "The Orchestra": "It is a design of a man / that makes [the birds] twitter. / It is a design," which seem to say that we perceive Nature through our own artifice—a position closer to that of Stevens's in "The Idea of Order at Key West"—Williams's sparrow is his own "man" so to speak, feistily improvising his lyrics even in the face of indifference or peril:

> He crouches
> before the female
> drags his wings,
> waltzing,
> throws back his head
> and simply—
> yells!

But females are dominant in sparrow mating, and Williams recounts once seeing a stunned male gripped by his crown-feathers and held precariously on the edge of a water pipe until a female bird "was through with him." "I laughed heartily," Williams tells us, seemingly familiar with the scenario.

At five-foot-nine, Williams was an average-sized man of outsized appetites. His comic poem "Smell" celebrates, via his nose, which he thought too large—"my hateful mirror / shows every day my big nose" ("Sappho, Be Comforted")— the pleasures and perils of his desires:

> Oh strong-ridged and deeply hollowed
> nose of mine! what will you not be smelling?
> What tactless asses we are, you and I, boney nose,
> . . . .
>   With what deep thirst
> we quicken our desires
> to that rank odor of a passing springtime!

Williams's sparrow, dropped by his lover, ends "flattened to the pavement," an "effigy of a sparrow." Yet the poet asserts that the "poem / of [the sparrow's] existence" triumphed nonetheless. Williams's end, even with the loss of his verbal powers, was neither as sudden nor as brutal. And one could do worse in describing his singular legacy in the American literary landscape than his portrait of this tenacious and lusty little bird, favored by the goddess of love:

>   his small size,
> keen eyes,
>   serviceable beak
>   and general truculence

*T*he plastic seed cup is full of nothing but empty husks. The water is dry. The paper at the bottom of the cage is rank. Poor Chet is desperate. I have neglected him. My heart races as I work quickly to fill his vessels with fresh food and water. I've barely secured the cup back onto the bars of his cage when he is upon it, his famished little frame shaking as he works madly with his beak to shell the seeds and eat his fill. I'm sickened with guilt, but also disoriented and confused: how could I have *forgotten* about Chet?

It's a dream. A repeated one my unconscious has deployed in the service of my unnerving, ever since Chet died. It happened while S. and I were living abroad. We had left him behind with our upstairs neighbor G., an old friend who had been in my life so long our friendship predated my relationship with S. We had figured out a way to bring our cat Circe to Paris, but we couldn't see how to do the same with our parakeet. Chet would fare, we thought, perfectly well for a brief year in the company of G., with whom he was already intimate. But Chet didn't make it.

Before G. moved to Providence, he and I had always lived in different cities and, but for the occasional in-person visit, we had conducted our friendship by letter. It suited me, for even before the muse came calling to calm the incessant pecking in my head, I was apprenticing to become a "man of letters" by essaying writerly *personae* in my correspondence. There were many unwitting recipients of these epistolary forays, though few showed interest in writing me back in the same spirit of *pretend* I required during that difficult metamorphosis from a person beholden to a family mythos to a belletristic sophisticate. G. was the exception. He always wrote back. He desired transformation as much as I did, and thus never mocked me in my little dramas. He even agreed to address me as "Frances Moxley" during an early attempt to distance myself from my historical moment, which was simply *glutted* with "Jennifers." A frivolous name, as I saw it.

G. was there when my first parakeet Emile died. I was speechless with grief. Inconsolable. He was staying with S. and me for a few months while he figured out a next step, and was scheduled to fly back to Seattle the next day. The bird's death backgrounded our preparations for his departure. He went into the kitchen and cooked me dinner. Fettuccine Alfredo. We sat on the couch eating the creamy, comforting pasta, watching a film I'd seen many times. Tears streamed down my face. The little bird was gone, the friend was going away. There was no need to talk.

Before S. took Emile's corpse to the woods to bury it, I saved one tiny blue chest feather. I put it in a ring box. I put the box in the dark confines of the top drawer of my Lady's Desk. It is there to this day. Of Chet I have only a list: a piece of paper torn from a yellow pad. On it, by my hand in black ink, are thirty phrases. Chet's vocabulary. When I look at these words my sadness is charmed by the memory of Chet's astonishing mimetic facility: from simple utterance to complex slang, he was the most verbal of budgies.

We acquired him in June of 1994, right after I completed my MFA. My cohort was decamping for distant corners, but since S. was still working on his doctorate, I would be staying put. Other methods of marking the change would have to be found. I decided that I would forego writing for an entire year. I would dedicate myself to reading, making up for my terrible California public-school education. I decided it was also time to try another bird.

Named for the great trumpet player Chet Baker, our new little budgie was petrified. When I approached the cage, his turquoise feathers would contract and he would stuff his little frame between the food and water dishes. Accustomed to Emile's gregariousness, I worried we'd adopted an asocial parakeet. I needn't have. By summer's end, Chet had grown bold and comfortable in his new digs. As S. recorded in his journal: "Jen read all of Malory's *Morte d'Arthur*, and in general has been keeping to her strict and ambitious plans for reading . . . I read less, due to writing, but we both watch numerous movies (of course). And Chet, our parakeet, has grown quite friendly and musical and, despite Circe's jealousy—which kicked in about a month ago—he's a lovely addition to daily living."

Chet had adopted the habit of letting out a chirp of joy whenever I came back to the apartment after a walk, grocery shopping, what have you. If I opened the cage, he would jump on my finger and stick out his beak for a pretend kiss. He liked lettuces and was vigorously aggressive with his toys: interlocking plastic rings that hung down, ending in a bell, a little rocking personage that he would punch and argue with. A mirror for romance. I affectionately teased him about being a "dirty bird" whenever I cleaned his cage.

Then one day G., S., and I were sitting on our living-room floor chatting and listening to music. Chet was keeping up his usually budgie badinage when S. distinctly heard him mix into his bird discourse the English phrase "dirty bird." We went silent, the better to listen, but Chet also, as if suddenly self-conscious, went silent too. We went back to talking, each with an ear attentive to the bird, and sure enough, we all distinctly heard Chet's English utterance: "dirty bird!" chirp, chirp, gurgle, whistle, chirrup, "dirty bird!"

Having revealed his facility for mimesis, I made an effort to punctuate my long bouts of reading by deliberately speaking certain words and phrases to Chet. He was a facile and enthusiastic learner. Every new expression seemed easier to impart than the previous. After "dirty bird," Chet learned to say, "poor John Keats," for I was reading the doomed poet's letters, and had begun to delve into W. Jackson Bate's biography. As for non-English phrases, Chet could say *buenos dias*, *mon petit oiseau*, *bonjour*, and, because in our quest to puzzle out the role of the writer in issues of social justice the Dreyfus affair was ever present: *J'accuse!* In addition to sweet nothings, such as "you're so cute," "what a handsome budgie," "gimme a kiss," and "I love you," there were literary winks such as "nevermore," "goodnight sweet prince," and the name "Walt Whitman." He liked to turn the free-verse champion into two iambs and an anapest, *Walt Whit, Walt Whit, Walt Whitman!*

I also taught Chet some novelty phrases and slang, such as "cup a joe," "thar' she blows," and, inspired by lingo I'd learned from the Coen Brothers' film *Miller's Crossing*, "Hey hep-cat, what's the rumpus?" This latter was, I believe, Chet's longest phrase and crowning achievement. One of the charms of his appropriations was his ability to improvise and interlace the human language with the bird, such that in between a run of gurgles and chirps you'd hear "*Buenos dias* sweet prince*,*" or "I love you Walt Whitman."

Having completed my year-long writing moratorium, I returned with fresh enthusiasm to the keyboard of my Selectric and wrote nascent drafts of what would eventually become *The Middle Room*, a memoir of my early literary development and the death of my parents. Chet preferred the steady sound made by prose to the long silences punctuated by pizzicatos characteristic of the way I wrote poetry, and he would chirp along. My work on *The Middle Room* had many false starts and fallow periods. By the time we were putting our things in storage before going abroad, there was still much work to be done. I had learned that, in writing about one's own past, memory is inadequate. You must also do research. And thus I set about gathering the resources I would need to finish the book while abroad, for I was still green enough to underestimate the time it would take to complete by about six years. My energy was high. I photocopied pages of my journal and selections from my correspondence to take with me. This is when it occurred to me that G.—who had moved back to Providence and now lived directly above us in the attic apartment—would have a trove of my letters from *exactly* the time in my life I was trying to reconstruct.

This was the first tear. I was breathless on the landing outside his door, excited. "Would you mind letting me have my letters back?" I rehearsed. As close friends between whom the many confidences ranged from dismal to giddy, my self-consciousness about this request was perturbing. *How self-involved! How solipsistic!* Such are the feelings every memoirist must rationalize. G. was the least and most judgmental of men. While unfailing in his support, he was also capable of little personal quips that came equipped with time-lapsed stings. But what happened when I asked G. about my letters was none of these things. What happened was, until it wasn't, unimaginable. G. said, "I can't return your letters because I threw them all away."

The destruction of the hand-written missives of youth by my most trusted and steady of interlocutors, at a time in my life when I was still smarting from the loss of so much I thought permanent, was news I would not recover from. G. could see I was upset. He pleaded ignorance of the value of literary things, but I knew that G., in his desire for transformation, often gutted his possessions. To him, retrospective glances provoked nausea, and the past was a seat of self-loathing. As far as I knew, our friendship had never experienced a rift so deep that one might, for example, burn letters out of hurt or anger. No, it wasn't that. "I just didn't understand that they were important to you," he said.

Not long after this exchange, S. and I were gone and Chet was installed in one of the cramped and dark attic rooms that G. had made his home. I cannot remember how long Chet endured this exile before, as G. reported, he started to go silent and seem unwell. Some construction the landlord undertook caused a fine black dust to cover everything. Perhaps it made the little bird sick with a form of silicosis or black lung. Birds are sensitive to fumes. As he had with Emile, S. held the view that Chet thought me his mate and that he died of longing when I left. This was the second tear. Though I knew G. was not responsible for Chet's death, I could not altogether rid myself of feeling hurt, not as by a sad happenstance, but as if a wrong had been done to me.

Returning to Paris helped me to look back into the past, the landscape an archive of memories in itself. Just like this soft, folded, cheap piece of yellow paper which I've kept for over twenty years. It includes no explanation or date, nor even Chet's name. It is just a list of thirty phrases, including "special budgie" and "feed the bird," which I keep forgetting to do and for which my unconscious will not forgive me.

"$\mathcal{B}$abe, turn around." I feel a rush of adrenaline. "Slowly." I'm at the baseline, in between points. S.'s changed posture indicates a shift in attention. My racket falls to my side and I turn around to see, in the copse behind the chain-link fence marking the borders of the tennis courts, a full-grown female deer. She is nonchalantly munching leaves, unperturbed by our game. I hear the rapid trill of a bird over-head. To me he sounds like a squeaky metal wheel. The doe's fluffy tail is chestnut-colored on top, white underneath. Like her ears, it twitches briskly against the bugs. How un-like the movement of human hands, I think.

I remember a story our realtor told us when we first moved to Maine. A well-loved and respected local man had mistaken a woman hanging up her laundry for a deer. He shot and killed her. She had been wearing white mittens which he mistook for a deer's tail. Though this detail was proffered as justification for the hunter's having mistaken one species for another, to me it only served to make the story stranger. Why was she hanging laundry outside on such a cold day? Wouldn't it be difficult to handle wet laundry wearing white mittens? Or were they gloves?

The nineteenth-century ballad "Polly Von" also turns on a hunter mistaking one species for another. A woman for a swan. I first heard "Polly Von" on Peter, Paul, and Mary's album *In the Wind*, which I bought used as a teen from Flip Side records for two dollars. I was very moved by the song, even though the premise struck me as outlandish. How could a woman be mistaken for a swan? As with the Maine killing, the accident is blamed on an article of clothing: "She'd her apron wrapped about her and he took her for a swan," the narrator tells us. Why was Polly outside in her apron? Was she, too, hanging out the laundry? Why does the seemingly innocuous detail of what a woman is wearing determine whether she will live or die?

According to the ballad, "the cruel hand of evil" undoes the hunter. His arrow seems possessed of a will apart: "And his true love was slain as the shaft found its mark." When he recognizes his mistake, the hunter feels shame and sadness: "He turned away his head for he could not bear to see / He lifted her up and found she was dead / A fountain of tears for his true love, he shed." In true ballad fashion, fate's cruel blows are not softened, not even by the cold comfort of a moral. There is no growth or change, only inexplicable tragedy.

The hunter takes Polly's body to "his home by the sea" and confesses to his father: "I've killed my fair love in the flower of her life! / I always intended that she'd be my wife." Searching for psychological comfort, the hunter returns to the scene of the accident. There he sees a lone swan gliding by. Is this meant to be Polly, metamorphosed into the beautiful bird she was mistaken for? The swan is indifferent to the hunter and he, having slain his true love, seems fated to a sad solitude.

Swans mate for life. And when their mates die, they grieve. This biological proclivity deepens the pathos of a pivotal scene in Richard Wagner's last opera, *Parsifal*, based on Wolfram von Eschenbach's thirteenth-century narrative, *Parzival*. Wagner introduces the opera's hero, an "innocent fool" who will eventually become the grail hero, by having him shoot down a swan. This is a displacement and alteration of an episode in the source text in which the young hero, while still under the care of his mother, Herzeloyde, cuts "bow and arrows with his own hands" and shoots at the "flocks of birds." His inherent moral potential is illustrated in his paradoxical relationship to his murderous impulses, for in Eschenbach's telling each time Parzival kills a bird, he "would burst into tears and, clutching at his hair, wreak vengeance on his own head." The swift transition he witnesses from "singing full throat" to lifeless silence devastates the young boy.

Parzival, who is "home schooled" by his mom in a secluded forest, "had no care in the world," Eschenbach tells us, "save the singing of the birds overhead." The songbirds arouse new and confusing feelings, their "sweetness pierced him to the heart and brought a tightness to his breast. All in tears he ran to [his mother]."

Parzival is unable to explain to her why he is so upset. She watches him carefully and one day notices that he is listening intently to "the happy clamour of the birds." Having realized that this is the source of her son's heartache, she recognizes that he is "the victim of amorous desire." Like the present-day mother who finds her tween watching porn, Herzeloyde reacts to this discovery grimly. She "turned her hatred on the birds" and she "ordered her ploughmen and drovers to hurry out and wring the necks of all the birds they could lay hands on!"

Wagner transforms Eschenbach's songbird-hunting episode into the swan shooting. Not just any swan, a sacred swan seeking his mate in the magical forest that surrounds the grail castle. The swan's motives are linked to the human actors, for in this place all creatures live in concert. In

Wagner's telling, Parsifal has no natural compassion, but needs to be schooled. "Whatever flies I can hit in flight!" he boasts when the sage grail knight Gurnemanz demands to know who has killed the swan. "What harm did that faithful swan do you?" Gurnemanz asks, "He was pleasing to us: what is he now to you? / Here look! Here you struck him, / the blood still congealing, the wings drooping lifeless, / the snowy plumage stained dark . . . How could you commit this crime?" By the time Gurnemanz has detailed the heinousness of Parsifal's act, the twelve-year-old hunter is a complete wreck. He breaks his bow and discards his arrows.

Unlike the tragic accident that results in Polly Von's death, Parsifal's killing of the swan is quite purposeful. It symbolizes his foolishness, which is born of his lack of empathy. In Stephane Mallarmé's sonnet "Vivacious, virginal, and beautiful day . . ." (*Le vierge, le vivace et le bel aujourd'hui*), often called "The Swan," the mute white bird, stuck in a frozen lake, symbolizes the impotent poet. The wingbeat of the present—a displacement of the frozen swan—acts as an analog for the poetic impulse.

Mallarmé's 1886 poem for Wagner, "Homage (to Wagner)," employs the same figure of the wingbeat he used in "Vivacious, virginal, and beautiful day . . ." There it is, in line seven, at the poem's dead center: "to deliver from the wingbeat a familiar thrill!" (*à propager de l'aile un frisson fam-*

ilier!). Mallarmé calls Wagner "a god" in his ambivalent "Homage" and, as if referring directly to *Parsifal,* which Wagner called a "stage-consecrated festival play," claims that the composer is "beaming a consecration" (*irradiant un sacre*).

"Since Wagner appeared, music and verse have combined to form Poetry," writes Mallarmé in *Crisis in Verse.* "The magnificence of words fade," he wrote to his uncle, "before the sunrise of contemporary Music, of which Wagner is the latest God." It is as if, for Mallarmé, Wagner's Parsifal has murdered not just *any* swan, but the divine Orpheus in his feathered incarnation as recounted in Plato's Vision of Er. The composer has ripped the lyre from the poet's hand and a new way of making poetic music must be found. The poet's "old triumphal struggle" (*vieil ébat triumphal*) is as impotent as a swan whose mate has been shot. The page must become a musical score capable of competing with Wagnerian staves. We are not so far off from *Un coup de dès...*

Perhaps the shadow of that same Orphic swan temporarily inhabited the fair form of Polly Von? Vivacious and virginal, her wings stretched above her apron strings in a triumphant apostrophe to the beautiful day, shot down "in the flower of her life," one lovely creature mistaken for another.

*F*or a long time when I read "The palm at the end of the mind," the first line of Wallace Stevens's poem "Of Mere Being," I saw not a tree but a hand. This is doubly odd in that the lofty venue wherein my juvenile poetic output first found its way to the public eye—the 1986 issue of University of California at San Diego's *Warren College Literary-Arts Journal*—appeared with a blurry and rather uncompelling black-and-white photograph of nine thin palm trees below the italicized all-caps title: *THE PALM AT THE END OF THE MIND*. They were taking that palm literally.

I remember the excitement I felt upon receiving that first and, what now seems to me, bizarrely verbose acceptance letter:

> This year the total number of submissions received by the editorial board for consideration was over one-hundred fifty. Since the size of the Journal is limited, only about twenty submissions could be accepted for publication. This constraint meant that only a selected number of pieces

could be included in the in the [sic] Journal. The determination as to which pieces would be included in the Journal was a difficult task. The final selections that the editorial board decided upon represent exceptional work. Those pieces selected for inclusion are, by any standards, quality works.

Good lord! And that is but *one* paragraph (out of three, and not the longest) typed with an electronic typewriter on Eaton's Corrasable Bond erasable paper, dated April 25, 1985 and sent to 3767 Albatross Street, where I was living with my parents. The compulsive repetition of the capitalized word "Journal" clothed in grandiosity what was essentially a very humble student-edited publication. I had sent in five poems, they had taken two, including the very first poem I'd ever written. It would never be so easy again.

At the time it did not occur to me that the capital-J journal's title, "The palm at the end of the mind," was a famous line from a famous poem by a famous poet. Very soon after I became a "published poet," Edwin Fussell— the very same professor who, in "Understanding Poetry," taught me that "Out of the Cradle Endlessly Rocking" followed the structure of Italian opera—introduced me to the poetry of Wallace Stevens. Stevens was a favorite of Fussell's. He taught the mid-length contemplative poems, "The Idea of Order at Key West" and "Sunday Morning," and that sonically comic oddity, "The Emperor of Ice Cream." Thus "Of Mere Being" would have to wait. I cannot recall the first time I read it, but there's a high probability it was in the mid-nineties, when I went through a passionate Stevens phase, devouring his letters and reading "Auroras of Autumn" and "The Comedian as the Letter C" aloud to myself with wonder and confusion.

Now that I am a professor of English at a public university, I teach a class very similar to "Understanding Poetry." In my first attempts, having had no pedagogical training, I copied Fussell's methods: cheeky weekly quizzes and a couple of mid-length papers analyzing a single poem. I taught "The Idea of Order at Key West." In the early days I would drag in a "boom box" and play a tape of Stevens's stentorian baritone rendition. S. and I always felt a thrill at the long pause Stevens inserts between the words "and singing" and the word "made" at the end of the third to last stanza. I would look out at the faces of my students and see them nodding off. The strains of Stevens's twentieth-century pacing acted as soporific. I had to evolve.

Now I teach "Of Mere Being" instead. It is short and just strange enough to provoke interesting conversation. I use it to teach tercets and symbol. In the "palm at the end of the mind" Stevens's "gold-feathered bird" "rises / In the bronze decor" and:

Sings in the palm, without human meaning,
Without human feeling, a foreign song.

You know then that it is not the reason
That makes us happy or unhappy.
The bird sings. Its feathers shine.

Then "the palm at the end of the mind" moves outside to "the edge of space," where the "wind moves slowly in the branches." Stevens concludes "Of Mere Being" with the image of a bird that rivals Yeats's Byzantine beauty: "The bird's fire-fangled feathers dangle down." Admitting so may expose me to censure, but each time I teach "Of Mere Being" I feel its enigmatic beauty anew. I have never bothered to check in with what the scholars are saying. I enjoy literary criticism, especially of an outdated stripe, so this obstinance has nothing to do with any anti-intellectual bias. And yet, there are times when mysteries are so very pleasant I feel loath to "solve" them.

Thus my irritation when a depressingly literal-minded student shattered "Of Mere Being" with a realist mallet by insisting that the poem was just a fancy description of a sunset on the beach. "It's obvious, 'fire-fangled feathers' is just describing the sun behind a palm tree," he said. He was being clever and expected a reward. As someone who is distressingly prone to missing the obvious, I looked down at the page with consternation. Hopefully I had the wherewithal to hide my private devastation and say something such as, "That's an interesting reading!" Just the kind, I feared, that the coerced roster of "Reading Poems" would cling to as a comforting solution to the frustrations I provoked by refusing to provide them with neat "answers" to the poems we struggled through.

But why was I, a promiscuous etymological adventurer fond of puzzling out linguistic questions, so resistant to seeking out Stevens's meaning in "Of Mere Being"? I felt an immediate kinship when Robert Creeley told an anecdote about a time when he and Robert Duncan were giving a talk on Charles Olson and they both went into raptures about his poem "The Binnacle." An audience member asked what a "binnacle" was. Creeley and Duncan looked at each other and realized that neither of them knew. Yet not knowing hadn't diminished their appreciation of the poem, or their love for that word, "binnacle." The word's foreignness and cadence were all of its allure, like the pleasures of Stevens's joyous rhyme of "fangled" with "dangle" at the end of "Of Mere Being."

The patness of the "sunset" solution seemed to me like a Google "top hit." It stopped thought from loitering in the neighborhood of the poem and put us back into the "mere" world: not the world of impossibility, of dreams and desires.

Not the palm at the end of the mind, but the palm on the cover of a greeting card, beautiful but lacking romance in inverse proportion to its attempt to conjure it. I wanted Stevens's fire-fangled gold-feathered bird to stay a mystery. A bird soul in the mind's tree singing a beautiful foreign song whose music, like that of the spheres on the edge of space, fills us with a disoriented longing for a beauty we do not have ears to hear.

Epigraphs: Pliny the Elder, *Naturalis Historia*, trans. John Bostock and H. T. Riley (London: Henry G. Bohn, 1855) on Perseus Digital Library, vol. 2, 510. Translation modified. / T. Rex, "Ride a White Swan," Fly, 1970.

BIRD SOUL

1: "without human meaning / Without human feeling": Wallace Stevens, "Of Mere Being" in *Collected Poetry and Prose* (New York: Library of America, 1997), 476.

2: "We are not chickadees / on a bare limb": William Carlos Williams, "To Daphne and Virginia" in *Pictures from Brueghel* (New York: New Directions, 1962), 77.

BLAST-BERUFFLED

3: Thomas Hardy, "The Darkling Thrush" in *The Complete Poems*, ed. James Gibson (New York: Macmillan, 1982), 150.

4: "dour October": James Schuyler, "The Bluet" in *Collected Poems* (New York: Farrar, Straus and Giroux, 1993), 196.

7: Walter Benjamin, "Some Motifs in Baudelaire" in *Charles Baude-laire, A Lyric Poet in the Era of High Capitalism,* trans. Harry Zohn (New York: Verso, 1992), 107–54. I draw on the entire essay, but the quotes can be found on 114–16.

8: Charles Baudelaire, "The Albatross," "The Swan," and "A Mar-tyr" in *The Flowers of Evil*, trans. James McGowan (Oxford, U.K.: Oxford University Press, 1998), 15, 173, 229.

SCHOOL FOR SONG

10: W. B. Yeats, "Sailing to Byzantium" in *The Poems of W. B. Yeats*, ed. Richard J. Finneran (New York: Macmillan, 1983), 193.

10: "Gather ye rosebuds": Robert Herrick, "To the Virgins, to make much of Time" in *The Complete Poetry of Robert Herrick,* ed. J. Max Patrick (New York: Anchor Doubleday, 1963), 117.

12: In Book VI of *The Aeneid* the Sybil of Cumae tells Aeneas that, if he would journey to the Underworld he must first break off a "golden bough . . . hidden upon a dark tree thick with leaves" to offer to Proserpina in the underworld. I've always had a fond-ness for the translation of Virgil's epic by L. R. Lind (Bloom-ington: Indiana University Press, 1962), as it was the first one that I read.

DEMI-BIRD

13: "Safe European Home" refers to a song by *The Clash* on their album *Give 'Em Enough Rope,* CBS Records, 1978.

14: Richard Eberhart, "The Groundhog" in *Selected Poems* (London: Chatto & Windus, 1951), 16–17.

15: Jennifer Moxley, "Fixed Idea" in *The Sense Record* (Washington, D.C.: Edge Books, 2002), 41–42.

16: "Yeats's entombed student lamp" refers to an image in his poem "The Leaders of the Crowd," in *The Poems of W. B. Yeats*, 184.

MY LOVE WAS A FEATHER

17: "My love was a feather": Robert Creeley, "The Whip" in *For Love: Poems 1950–1960* (New York: Scribners, 1962), 51.

17: John Keats, "Ode to a Nightingale" in *Poetical Works,* ed. H. W. Garrod (Oxford, U.K.: Oxford University Press, 1956), 207–9.

18: Moxley, "Little Brick Walk" in *The Sense Record*, 49–51.

19: Robert Creeley, "Old Poems" in *Life and Death* (New York: New Directions, 1998), 62.

20: Edwin Arlington Robinson, "The Man Against the Sky" in *Collected Poems* (New York: Macmillan, 1922), 60–69.

THE WEARINESS, THE FEVER, AND THE FRET

22: Keats, "Ode to a Nightingale" in *Poetical Works*, 207–9.

22: *The Dead*, directed by John Huston, Vestron Pictures, 1987.

23: "The repeated cry of the bird is *oci, oci, oci . . .* the imperative of the Old French verb *occir,* and the call, therefore is 'kill, kill, kill,'" writes J. L. Baird in his introduction to *Rossignol* (Kent, Ohio: Kent State University Press, 1978), 19–29, explaining how some medieval writers correlated the nightingale's springtime song with the time when kings go out to war. Furthermore, this "view of the bird as a reminder of or inciter to violence . . . is, of course, a purely medieval development, since it depends on word-play in the cry of the bird not available to the classical poet."

23: Keats, "Bright Star" in *Poetical Works*, 372.

23: Michael Clune, *Writing against Time* (Palo Alto, Cal.: Stanford University Press, 2013), 4–6.

24: My discussion of *Philomela querens* is indebted to Baird's scholarship in his introduction to *Rossignol*.

24: Ovid *Metamorphoses* 6.196–204.

PHILOMELA QUERENS

25: Ovid, *Metamorphoses*, trans. Allen Mandelbaum (New York: Harcourt Inc., 1993), 91.

26: Edith Hamilton, *Mythology* (New York: New American Library, 1969).

28: "*queritur / antiqua de iactura*" are lines from *Carmina Burana*, quoted in the introduction to *Rossignol*, 5–6.

SOME ARE BORN TO ENDLESS NIGHT

29: Keats, "Ode on a Grecian Urn" in *Poetical Works*, 209.

29: Ovid, *Metamorphoses*, trans. Mandelbaum, 223.

29: Virgil, *Georgics*, trans. L. P. Wilkinson (London: Penguin, 1982), 141–42.

31: Hesiod, *Works and Days*, trans. Apostolos N. Athanassakis (Baltimore, Md.: John Hopkins University Press, 1983), 72.

31: "drowsy Emperor awake": Yeats, "Sailing to Byzantium" in *The Poems of W. B. Yeats*, 193.

DEMON OR BIRD!

33: Walt Whitman, "Out of the Cradle Endlessly Rocking" in *The Complete Poems,* ed. Francis Murphy (New York: Penguin, 1975), 275–81.

35: "powerful feelings recollected in tranquility" is William Wordsworth's description of how poets access their emotional experiences in order to transform them into poems in his 1801 *Preface to Lyrical Ballads.*

36: Virgil, *Georgics*, trans. Wilkinson, 142.

36: Whitman, "Song of Myself" in *The Complete Poems*, 63–124.

37: "given that the first three Renaissance musical works we have come to call 'operas' all took the myth of Orpheus and Eurydice as their subject matter": these three works are Jacobo Peri's *Euridice* (1600), libretto by Ottavio Rinuccini; Guilio Caccini's *Euridice* (1600) (same libretto); and the most famous, Monteverdi's *Orfeo* (1607), libretto by Alessandro Striggio. I wrote at greater length about Orpheus and these works in a blog entry titled "Orpheus and Opera, A Love Story," posted at jennifermoxley.com on 20 June 2016.

THE ALL-DAY BIRD

38: Denise Levertov, "Claritas" and "Say the Word" in *Poems 1960–1967* (New York: New Directions, 1983), 107–8 and 113–19.

39: Levertov, "Some Notes on Organic Form" in *New and Selected Essays* (New York: New Directions, 1992), 67–73.

42: Gerard Manley Hopkins, "Binsey Poplars" in *Poems and Prose*, ed. W. H. Gardner (New York: Penguin, 1985), 40.

EASY AS A STAR

44: Emily Dickinson, 445 in *The Poems of Emily Dickinson,* ed. R. W. Franklin (Cambridge, Mass.: Belknap / Harvard, 1999), 206.

IN SERVICE

56: Rainer Maria Rilke's ideas about the adjacent "two solitudes," and a child's "wise not-understanding," can be found in his *Letters to a Young Poet,* trans. Stephen Mitchell (New York: Modern Library, 2001), 78, 55.

57: Robert Baldick, introduction to his translation of Gustave Flaubert's *Three Tales* (London: Penguin, 1961), 7.

57: "I worked for sixteen hours . . ." comes from Flaubert's Letter to Madame Roger de Genettes, 13–18 March 1876 (my translation).

57: Flaubert, "A Simple Heart" in *Three Tales*, 17.

57: "the word that corresponds . . .": Ezra Pound, *The ABC of Reading* (New York: New Directions, 1960), 88.

58: "I'm regarded as one of its high priests"; "mixture of beautiful and ugly . . .": *The Letters of Gustave Flaubert 1857–1880,* ed. and trans. by Francis Steegmuller (Cambridge, Mass.: Belknap/Harvard, 1982), 231, 230.

58: "only emotion endures": Pound, "A Retrospect" in *The Literary Essays of Ezra Pound,* ed. T. S. Eliot (New York: New Directions, 1954), 14.

59: Flaubert, "A Simple Heart," 49–50.

60: ibid., 30, 52.

61: "odi et amo" refers to the opening of Catullus's poem 85 and translates as "I hate and I love."

62: "good art as the high mass is good art": Pound, *The Spirit of Romance* (New York: New Directions, 2005), 89.

62: John Cowper Powys, *The Religion of a Skeptic* (New York: Dodd, Mead and Company, 1925), 42.

62: Robert Duncan, *The H. D. Book* (Berkeley: University of California Press, 2011), 63.

63: Edgar Allen Poe, "The Philosophy of Composition" in *Essays and Reviews* (New York: Library of America, 1984), 18.

64: Flaubert, "A Simple Heart," 47, 45.

65: Moxley, "Invective Verse" in *o·blēk* 12: Writing from the New Coast (1993): 182–83.

THE SWIFTS

67: Shakespeare *Macbeth* 2.3.49–50.

71: Douglas Oliver, *Whisper 'Louise'* (Hastings, U.K.: Reality Street, 2005).

72: Mary Webb, *Precious Bane* (New York: Modern Library, 1928), 44–45.

73: T. S. Eliot, "Hamlet" in *Selected Essays* (London: Faber and Faber, 1986), 141–46.

75: Robert Pogue Harrison, *The Dominion of the Dead* (Chicago: University of Chicago Press, 2003), 1.

PIGEON

80: Todd Telander, *Birds of Virginia,* a Falcon Field Guide (Guilford, Conn.: Morris Book Publishing, 2013), 44.

NO MORE SHE MOURNS

84: George Frideric Handel, *Acis and Galatea,* chamber version of 1718, libretto by John Gay, Alexander Pope, and John Hughes.

84: All quotations of the libretto are taken from the *Boston Early Music Festival 2009–2010* concert series program, which uses the text of *Acis and Galatea: a mask, set to music by Mr. Handel*, ed. Clifford Bartlett (Huntingdon, U.K.: King's Music, 1988).

84: "unfinished" simile is scholar Dianne Dugaw's claim in *Deep Play: John Gay and the Invention of Modernity* (Newark: University of Delaware Press, 2001), 150.

84: Richard O. Prum, *The Evolution of Beauty* (New York: Anchor Books, 2017), 28, 82.

85: "the scholarly habit of attributing . . .": David Nokes, *John Gay: A Profession of Friendship* (Oxford, U.K.: Oxford University Press, 1995), 276, n. 31.

86: Ovid, Book XIII of *Metamorphoses*, trans. Sir Samuel Garth, John Dryden, et al., The Internet Classics Archive, http://classics.mit.edu/Ovid/metam.html.

86: "My quest to uncover *which* words are Gay's, which Pope's, and which Hughes's . . .": The best source on this question is Brian Trowell's essay "*Acis, Galatea and Polyphemus*: a 'serenata a tre voci?'" in *Music and Theatre: Essays in honour of Winton Dean* (Cambridge, U.K.: Cambridge University Press, 1987), 31–94.

86: "One source cited Pope's *Pastorals*": This claim was made by Ellen T. Harris, *Boston Early Music Festival 2009–2010* concert series program.

86: Alexander Pope, *The Poems of Alexander Pope,* ed. John Butt (New Haven, Conn.: Yale University Press, 1963), 119–38.

87: René Rapin, *The Idylliums of Theocritus with Rapin's Discourse of Pastorals Done into English* (Oxford, 1684), 7.

87: "One scholar charmingly calls this pathetic fallacy the shepherd's catalog of 'entitlements'": Dugaw, *Deep Play: John Gay and the Invention of Modernity*, 147.

88: Charles Darwin, *The Descent of Man, and Selection in Relation to Sex* (London: John Murray, 1871), 516.

88: Ronan Farrow, "From Aggressive Overtures to Sexual Assault: Harvey Weinstein's Accusers Tell Their Stories" on *newyorker .com*, 10 October 2017.

89: "In an earlier version . . .": Trowell, "*Acis, Galatea and Polyphemus*: a 'serenata a tre voci?,'" 54.

BIRD OF PARADISE

94: Robert Adamson, *Inside Out, An Autobiography* (Sydney: Text Publishing, 2004).

95: Cornell Lab of Ornithology, https://www.birds.cornell.edu/ home/

97: Moxley, "Three Graces" in *Imagination Verses* (New York: Tender Buttons, 1996), 73–74.

100: Moxley, "Enlightenment Evidence" in *Often Capital* (Chicago: Flood Editions, 2005). The group translation of it into French was published as *Evidence des Lumières*, trans. Julliette Valéry et al. (France: Editions Créaphis, 1998).

ON THE STREET WHERE YOU LIVE

104: My title refers to a song from the Lerner and Loewe musical *My Fair Lady.*

104: Hilda Doolittle (H. D.), *Collected Poems 1912–1944*, ed. Louis L. Martz (New York: New Directions, 1986), 568.

107: Fred Bodsworth, *Last of the Curlews* (Berkeley, Cal.: Counterpoint, 1995), 22, 18, 22.

108: ibid., 42.

109: Moxley, "The Fountain" in *Clampdown* (Chicago: Flood Editions, 2009), 5–8.

110: "Coyness, as Marvell knew": Andrew Marvell, "To His Coy Mistress."

110: Bodsworth, *Last of the Curlews*, 81–82.

110: The Ann Lauterbach poem is "Cheer" in *Spell* (New York: Penguin, 2018), 50–51.

MY HUMAN SOUL

112: Duncan, "My Mother Would Be a Falconress" and "A Lammas Tiding" in *Bending the Bow* (New York: New Directions, 1968), 51–54.

114: T. H. White, *The Goshawk* (New York: Putnam, 1951).

115: Moxley, *Imagination Verses*, x.

116: "conflicting loyalties": I also wrote about this episode in my memoir, *The Middle Room* (Berkeley, Cal.: Subpress, 2007).

119: "appalling destiny": I remember once being told that Robert Duncan described the vocation of a poet as an "appalling destiny," but I have been unable to trace the source, so this may be apocryphal.

WOMAN OR SWAN

120: Plato, *The Republic of Plato*, trans. Allan Bloom (New York: Basic Books, 1968), 297–303.

122: Alfred Lord Tennyson, "The Dying Swan," line 29, in *Tennyson's Poetry*, ed. Robert W. Hill Jr. (New York: W.W. Norton and Co., 1999), 28.

122: For a full account of the Orphic Theogony, see W. K. C. Guthrie, *Orpheus and Greek Religion* (Princeton, N.J.: Princeton University Press, 1993), 78–83.

122: Apollonius of Rhodes, *The Argonautica*, in *Hellenistic Poetry*, trans. Barbara Hughes Fowler (Madison: University of Wisconsin Press, 1990), 86–87.

123: William Rimmer, *Evening (The Fall of Day)*, 1870, crayon, oil and graphite on canvas, Boston Museum of Fine Arts.

123: Ovid *Metamorphoses* 10.328.

126: Rapin, *The Idylliums of Theocritus*, 7.

126: D. H. Lawrence, *Birds, Beasts and Flowers* (London: Martin Secker, 1923), 141–51.

129: Duncan, "Man's Fulfillment in Order and Strife" in *Collected Essays and Other Prose,* ed. James Maynard (Berkeley: University of California Press, 2004), 223.

MAX THE BIRDMAN

132: Keith and Rosmarie Waldrop, *Ceci n'est pas Keith—Ceci n'est pas Rosmarie: Autobiographies* (Providence, R.I.: Burning Deck, 2002), 19.

133: Keith Waldrop, *The Real Subject: Queries and Conjectures of Jacob Delafon with Sample Poems* (Richmond, Cal.: Omnidawn, 2004).

135: The black-and-white version of the image in the poster I describe can be found in Max Ernst's *Une Semaine de bonté: A Surrealistic Novel in* Collage (New York: Dover, 1976), 141.

136: Paul Éluard, "Max Ernst" in *Capitale de la douleur* (Paris: Gallimard, 1966), 13.

THE SPARROW

138: Sappho translations come from: *Poems and Fragments,* trans. Stanley Lombardo (Indianapolis, Ind.: Hackett Publishing Co., 2002); *If Not, Winter: Fragments of Sappho,* trans. Anne Carson (New York: Vintage, 2003); *Sappho*, trans. Mary Barnard (Berkeley: University of California Press, 1958); and *Greek*

Lyrics, trans. Richmond Lattimore (Chicago: University of Chicago Press, 1960).

138: "simple question of weight ratio." The writer of this note has been sacked.

139: Catullus, *The Poems of Catullus,* trans. Peter Whigham (New York: Penguin, 1966), 10, 51.

141: Williams, "Sappho, Be Comforted," "The Sparrow," and "The Orchestra" in *Pictures from Brueghel,* 65, 129–132, 82.

142: Stevens, "The Idea of Order at Key West" in *Collected Poetry and Prose,* 105–6.

143: Williams, "Smell" in *The Collected Poems of William Carlos Williams, Vol I: 1909–1939,* ed. A. Walton Litz and Christopher MacGowan (New York: New Directions, 1986), 92.

CHET

149: W. Jackson Bate, *John Keats* (Cambridge, Mass.: Harvard University Press, 1963).

VIVACIOUS, VIRGINAL, AND BEAUTIFUL DAY

154: "Polly Von" (traditional) on Peter, Paul and Mary, *In the Wind,* Warner Bros., 1963.

155: Wolfram von Eschenbach, *Parzival,* trans. A. T. Hatto (New York: Penguin, 1980), 71.

157: Stephane Mallarmé, *Oeuvres complètes,* ed. Bertrand Marchal (Paris: Gallimard, 1998), 36–37, 39. The translations are mine.

158: Mallarmé, *Selected Prose Poems, Essays, and Letters,* trans. Bradford Cook (Baltimore, Md.: Johns Hopkins University Press, 1956), 39.

158: "'The magnificence of words fade,' he wrote to his uncle" is quoted in *Stephane Mallarmé: The Poems in Verse*, trans. Peter Manson (Miami, Ohio: Miami University Press, 2012), 258.

A FOREIGN SONG

161: Stevens, "Of Mere Being" in *Collected Poetry and Prose*, 476–77.

ACKNOWLEDGMENTS

Thank you to Nathaniel Mackey for publishing "Bird Soul," "Demi-bird," "My Love Was a Feather," and "*Philomela Querens*" in *Hambone* 22; and to David Trinidad and Tony Trigilio for publishing "Pigeon" and "My Human Soul" in *Court Green* 17. The title of this book is a slogan on "Useful Birds of America" trading cards, published by Church & Dwight Company, makers of Arm & Hammer and Cow Brand baking soda.